Grace

May God
Many years.
Congratulations on your
Graduation!
Love Mrs Grambush

M000170074

© 2014 Rockport Publishers

First published in the United States
of America in 2014 by
Rockport Publishers, a member
of Quarto Publishing Group USA Inc.
100 Cummings Center
Suite 406-L
Beverly, Massachusetts 01915-6101
Telephone: (978) 282-9590
Fax: (978) 283-2742
www.rockpub.com
Visit RockPaperInk.com to share your opinions,
creations, and passion for design.

All rights reserved. No part of this book may be
reproduced in any form without written permission
of the copyright owners. All images in this book
have been reproduced with the knowledge and
prior consent of the artists concerned, and no
responsibility is accepted by producer, publisher,
or printer for any infringement of copyright
or otherwise, arising from the contents of this
publication. Every effort has been made to ensure
that credits accurately comply with information
supplied. We apologize for any inaccuracies that
may have occurred and will resolve inaccurate or
missing information in a subsequent reprinting of
the book.

10 9 8 7 6 5 4 3 2

ISBN: 978-1-59253-902-4

Digital edition published in 2014
eISBN: 978-1-62788-054-1

A bibliography for this book appears online.
Go to rockpub.com/pages/paper-cut.

Library of Congress Cataloging-in-Publication Data
available

Cover Image: Owen Gildersleeve
Design: Chris Clarke and Owen Gildersleeve
Typset in: Gilderserif, Mercury and Replica

Printed in China

PAP ER CUT

**An Exploration into
the Contemporary
World of Papercraft
Art and Illustration**

Rockport Publishers
100 Cummings Center, Suite 406L
Beverly, MA 01915

rockpub.com • rockpaperink.com

Owen Gildersleeve

Preface

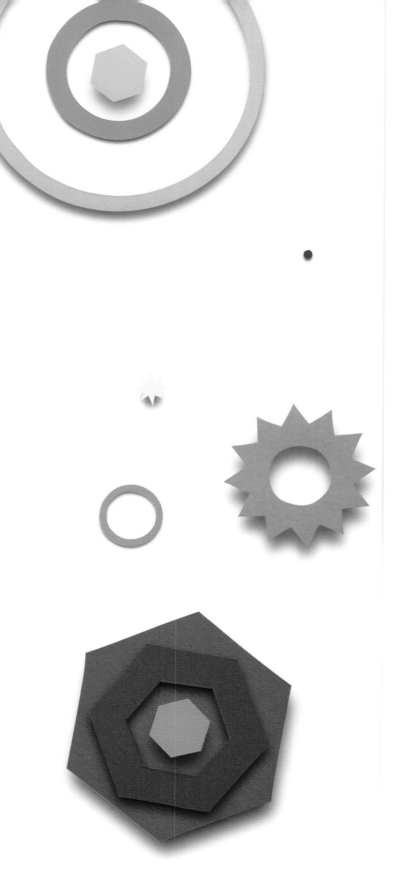

Many books have explored the subject of papercraft illustration, but few have really delved into the working lives of the artists involved. As an illustrator who often works with paper, I am aware of how much thought and preparation goes into creating these works, with the final image showing only a small fraction of the story. What makes these artists tick? How did they get into this field of illustration, and why do they work with paper? What is it about their work that makes them unique?

By looking at a handpicked selection of twenty-five of the world's leading papercraft artists, I have set out to answer these questions. Some of these artists are good friends whom I have met through my work over the years, and others I will be meeting for the first time for the purposes of this book; all are artists I greatly respect and admire. Through in-depth interviews and rarely published behind-the-scenes imagery, I hope to find out more about their individual crafts, giving a unique insight into the contemporary world of papercraft art and illustration.

Contents

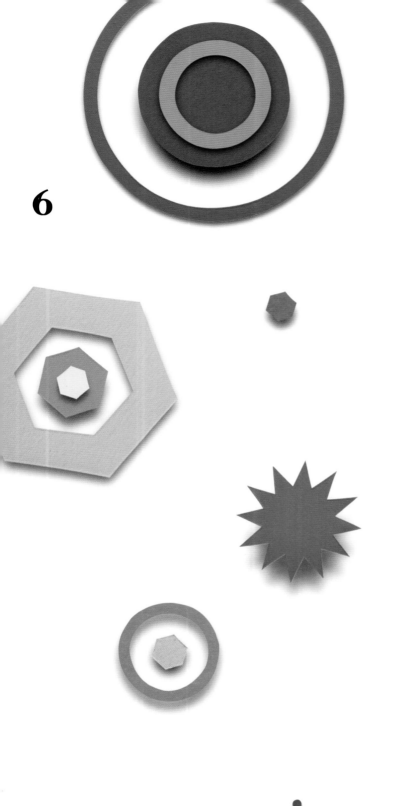

Introduction

Over the past few years, some of you might have noticed a backward shift in the world of design, toward the more handmade physical form. Billboards, magazines, and websites that were once plastered with digital imagery are now being replaced with pictures of physical, handcrafted illustrations and sets. With this resurgence has also come a shift toward paper-based illustration, and there are now countless books, websites, and blogs focusing on the art of paper-cutting. But what is it about paper that has made it such a popular artistic medium, and why is this resurgence happening now?

In a world that's become saturated with faultless digital design, the importance of human interaction and its inherent imperfections has become hugely important. We want to feel a connection with the imagery we are looking at, and even if it's just a photograph of the finished illustration, knowing that it exists as a physical artwork is hugely satisfying.

We are meant to create with our hands, and so by moving back toward a handcrafted way of working, we are consciously breaking free of the shackles of the digital age in which we live, where our creativity is restrained by the limitations of the programs available to us.

Although there is a large range of media being used in this new wave of tactile image-making and design, paper seems to be the most popular of the materials. One reason for its popularity is that, unlike metal, wood, or textiles, paper is cheap and so easily replaceable that artists never need to be afraid of spoiling it.

This leads to the ultimate freedom of artistic expression, where the artist has no boundaries or restraints. As a material, it is also extremely light and durable and can be folded and cut into any shape imaginable, leading to an infinite array of uses, which is why the range of artwork in this book is so broad and varied.

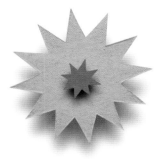

A Brief History

It would be fair to say that paper is one of the most important inventions in the development of human civilization. Over the millennia, it has helped humanity to spread information across the globe through printed text and imagery, allowing communication across cultures. This has been possible due to the amazing flexibility of the material. Being as inexpensive and accessible as it is, paper makes the perfect tool for the mass production of images and the written word.

It all began in China, during the Eastern Han Dynasty in the first century BCE, when a Chinese eunuch named Cai Lun invented what we now consider paper. Although forms of the material had existed before, Lun's version contained essential new materials that significantly improved its durability and production. This paper was created using a process in which fibers of bark, hemp, and silk were suspended in water. A sieve-like screen would then be used to gather the fibers, and this pulp would dry into a thin, matted sheet. Over the course of the next 2,000 years, the craft and tools used have become far more complex, but the basic principle and process remains the same.

Initially, this paper was exclusively the preserve of the imperial courts, but over time, its production spread to the wider population of China. The material was predominantly used for letter writing and transcribing scripture, but it also had great potential as a creative medium for recreational purposes. It is around this time that paper-cutting first appeared, when the Chinese used paper to create decorations for festivals and other celebrations. A popular custom was to cut paper into small banners, butterflies, and pieces of money, to place in women's hair at the beginning of spring. The technique was also used to create scenes and decorations for people's homes, sometimes featuring imagery of plants, flowers, birds, and animals. Symbols of good luck were also popular: the peach and pine for long life, the pomegranate for many children, and the melon for a rich harvest. Farm women would work on cuttings in their leisure time, sometimes creating large landscapes featuring imagery of cattle, weaving, fishing, and tilling. Paper-cutting also appeared in a number of Chinese writings, including a poem by the prominent Tang Dynasty poet Tu Fu, who said, "I cut paper to summon my souls."

In the sixth century, the art of paper-cutting began to spread east out of China with the Buddhist monks into Vietnam and Tibet, and then into Japan. Here the art form developed into *kirigami*, which is a mixture of origami and paper-cutting. Typically, *kirigami* starts with a single sheet of paper that is folded a number of times and then cut into. This sheet is then opened and flattened to reveal the finished artwork. Due to the nature of the art form, this technique lends itself well to creating symmetrical patterns, and artworks often featured imagery such as snowflakes, pentagrams, or orchid blossoms. Another art form developed called *monkiri*, which translates as "crest-cutting." This was used in a similar manner to kirigami, to cut out family emblems to decorate the home.

By the eighth century, the art form had started to spread west along a 4,000-mile-long network of trade routes that stretched all the way through the Middle East and into the outer reaches of Europe: the Silk Road. In India, paper-cutting was used for *sanjih*, a ritualistic craft used in the worship of Lord Krishna. This involved cutting intricate stencils depicting scenes from the life of the god, which were used to make decorative patterns on the living room or courtyard floors, called *rangolis*, welcoming the Hindu deities. In the 1300s, paper-cutting also began to appear in Israel, used by the Jewish community to create intricate religious artifacts such as *Mizrachs*—small ornamental plaques placed in the home to indicate the direction of prayer—and decorations for the Jewish holiday of Shavuot.

At the end of the fifteenth century, paper-cutting reached Europe, first in countries such as Ukraine and Poland, where pieces were initially created by the upper classes for sealing private letters. Later, as paper became cheaper and more accessible, the art form spread into the countryside. Ordinary farm workers would make highly decorative pieces called *vytynanky* or *wycinanki* for their homes and for religious celebrations, which represented stylized figures of people, animals, and plants. Paper-cutting gradually made its way farther into Europe, with examples appearing in Switzerland and Germany in the sixteenth century called *scherenschnitte*, meaning "scissor cut." These were traditionally created with black and white paper using symmetrical shapes and silhouetted forms.

Rob Ryan's intricate pape-cuts are inspired by traditional Polish *Wycicananki* featuring highly decorative forms and layouts.

This art form was later brought over to colonial America by eighteenth-century immigrants who settled in Pennsylvania, beginning a whole new wave of paper-cutting in North America that still exists today.

Another German tradition was to create prettily cut-out letters called *bindebrevs* (binding letters) that were sent out to loved ones on their birthdays. These contained a verse with an almost unsolvable riddle, which was decorated with hearts, cupids, and flowers. If the recipient did not solve the riddle before the sun went down, he or she was required to hold a feast. This tradition later passed on to Norway and Denmark, where it has developed into the present-day *gækkebrev*: a form of love letter that is given at Easter.

The famous Danish author and poet Hans Christian Andersen is best remembered for his fairy tales. But he also had a passion for paper-cutting and was never without a small pair of scissors that he kept together with his pen. In a letter written to his friend in 1867, he said: "Cutting is the fledgling beginning of poetry." He would often give readings of his poetry while simultaneously creating a paper-cutting. When the reading had finished, he would open and reveal the finished paper-cut to the delight of the audience.

The mid-nineteenth century marked a big step forward in the production of paper, with the process becoming mechanized. This increased production speed helped to keep up with the increasing demand for paper as both craft and reading materials, and in turn allowed for its widespread use worldwide. From then on, paper could be acquired extremely cheaply, making it an even more desirable medium for arts and crafts purposes.

Around this time in Mexico, laborers would purchase all their necessities from what were known as hacienda stores. As well as stocking day-to-day items, these stores stocked *papel de China*—known as *tissue paper* in English—and the workers began to use this type of paper to create elaborate decorations for their festivals. These artworks became known as *papel picado*, meaning "punched paper," because they were, and still are to this day, created using a hammer and chisel to cut into multiple sheets of paper, sometimes up to fifty sheets at a time. Although the art form had existed in Mexico before this time, the low cost and accessibility of the tissue paper led to a massive resurgence in the craft. Papel picado will often depict flowers and skeletons and are most commonly used for celebrations such as the Day of the Dead.

Over the course of the twentieth century, many new practitioners started to delve into the practice of paper-cutting, while the existing traditional forms continued to flourish. The artist Henri Matisse devoted the last fourteen years of his life to creating large-scale paper-cuts. Initially a painter and sculptor, Matisse was wheelchair-bound following surgery for cancer. After his illness, he found a new outlet for his creativity in paper-cutting, describing this time as "a second life." The bold and expressive nature of these paper-cuttings led to what some call the most influential and admired period of his career.

Contemporary Papercraft

At the same time as Matisse was creating paper-cut artworks such as *The Snail* in the late 1940s, graphic design and illustration was experiencing a new lease on life. As people were striving to push forward economically at the end of World War II, there was a greater need for advertising and packaging, especially in America with its booming economy. Events such as the Festival of Britain in 1951 also helped to promote design, architecture, and the arts in these postwar times, showcasing them to an audience of more than 10 million visitors. During these decades, there were also major advancements in computing. Early mechanical analog computers,

which originated in the 1940s, were gradually becoming faster and more powerful. Soon these machines were small enough for people to have in their homes.

By the 1990s, with further advances in digital media and the birth of the Internet, paper became somewhat redundant as a means of communication. Emails largely took over from written letters, printed newspapers began to be replaced by their online versions, and advertising became a lot more focused on digital solutions. This in turn had a big effect on design and illustration, with artists moving away from handcrafted image-making to a more digital style where cuts and folds were replaced by pixels and vectors.

But in recent years, there has been somewhat of a resurgence in handcrafted illustration. People have begun to shrug off the clean and polished vector styles, and once again embrace the imperfections of handcrafted illustration. In turn, this has led to artists once more developing a more personal relationship with their materials, and due to the versatility of paper as an expressive medium, it has again found itself at the heart of this creative renaissance.

But unlike paper-cutting of the past, this new wave has risen in tandem with digital media, and so the two are strongly interlinked. To a large degree, the way papercraft is used today relies heavily on digital means; some artists use digital devices to cut out their artwork, and others rely heavily on digital manipulation after the image has been photographed. Some artists rely purely on digital methods to create artworks that appear handmade; Eiko Ojala (page 136) only uses paper and shadows as a reference for his digital artworks.

Digital photography has also played a key part in this resurgence. In order for handcrafted illustrations and sets to be used for creative jobs, they often need to be photographed so that they can then be applied to adverts or used in magazines, newspapers, or online. Before the days of digital photography, this was a very laborious and often expensive process, making quick turnarounds almost impossible. But advances in digital photography have meant that handmade sets can be shot and edited in a single day, making this type of illustration more feasible for editorial jobs and advertising campaigns with quick turnarounds. A decent camera can now be bought relatively

cheaply, meaning that artists are now able to photograph their own work and take charge of the whole project if they so desire. Photographer Elise (featured on page 46) is one example of an artist who embodies this approach, playing the part of set designer, photographer, and retoucher in her projects.

The Internet has also played a big part in promoting papercraft. Styles that once were exclusive to a specific culture in one part of the world are now being combined and developed with other techniques, creating new and unique approaches to paper-cutting. Marc Hagan-Guirey (page 73) exemplifies this: an artist who is born and raised in the UK but whose work is inspired by the traditional Japanese technique of kirigami. Furthermore, paper is no longer being seen as just a 2-D building material and is now being used to create large 3-D illustrations, sets, and installations. Kyle Bean (page 18), Chrissie Macdonald (page 84), and Hattie Newman (page 121) all play with scale and three-dimensional forms. You can now see examples of papercraft illustration wherever you go, from large billboard advertising campaigns, to magazine covers, book jackets, and packaging designs. Its rise in popularity as an art form has led to some artists acquiring worldwide fame and admiration; leading practitioners Rob Ryan (page 148), Yulia Brodskaya (page 26), and Jeff Nishinaka (page 129) are all featured in this book.

Elise's work crosses the boundaries between set design and photography embracing the advances in digital technology.

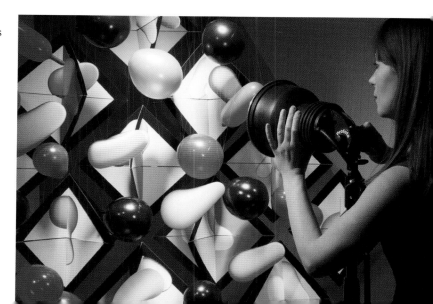

Andersen M Studio
Yulia Brodskaya Bia
Le Creative Sweatsh
Alexis Facca Helen
Mayuko Fujino Mar
Lobulo Chrissie Mac
The Makerie Stuart
Motherbird Helen M
Hattie Newman Jeff
Eiko Ojala Ciara Ph
Rob Ryan Shotopop
Fideli Sundqvist Zim

yle Bean

nca Chang

pp Elise

riel

Hagan-Guirey

Ionald

McLachlan

usselwhite

Nishinaka

lan

Mandy Smith

& Zou

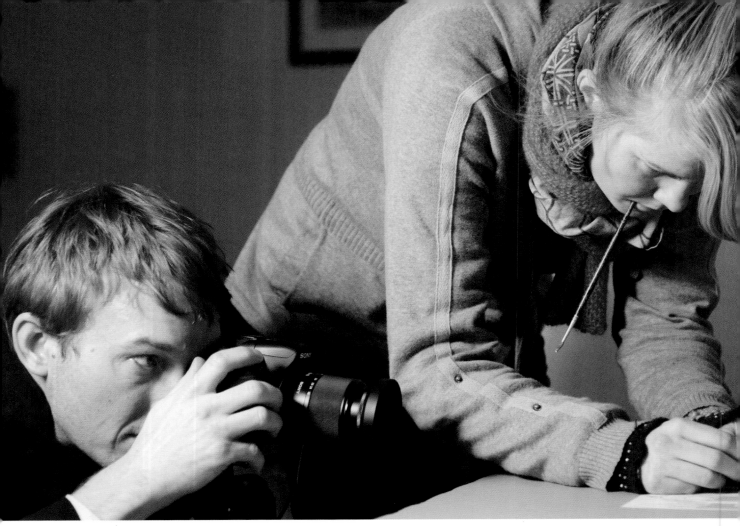

Star Alliance
Martin and Line of
Andersen M Studio
working on an animation
for Star Alliance created
out of airline tickets.

Andersen M Studio comprises siblings Martin and Line Andersen who work together from their studio in London to produce original and exciting creative communications. The studio works in a number of disciplines, from graphic design to beautifully detailed paper-cut stop-frame animations, often bringing book page fantasies to life. The duo have produced commercial pieces for clients such as Cartier, Nokia, and Channel 4, and their incredible stop-frame animation "Going West" has earned them a number of prestigious awards, including two Cannes Gold Lions.

13
London
UK

Martin, can you tell us a little bit about how Andersen M Studio came about?

We are from a small fishing town in Denmark called Sønderborg. We both moved to London to study visual communication design and both graduated with a M.A.: me from the Royal College of Art (1998) and Line from Central Saint Martins (2006). I worked for two years with Vaughan Oliver and Chris Bigg designing music packaging, before setting up Andersen M Studio in 2001.

Upon graduation in 2006, Line won the Creative Futures Award for her design work, and later that year, she joined Andersen M Studio, creating an interesting creative partnership between us because we specialize in different disciplines (me in typography and photography, and Line in stop-frame animation and hand-drawn typeface design). Over the past seven years, we have worked side by side on almost all projects that have come our way, including stop-frame animations, designing photography books and music packaging, brand identities, typography, films, and music. The studio has grown to become multidisciplinary.

What led you to start using paper in your work, and what is it about the material that attracts you to keep using it?

We have both always been very hands-on with our work, and craftsmanship is very much part of what defines Andersen M Studio. We started creating paper animations back in 2006. Line had made a paper animation as part of her M.A. graduation show at

Andersen M Studio

Going West
Stills from an stop-
frame animation for
the New Zealand Book
Council, which won 2
Gold Lions at Cannes.

Central Saint Martins in 2006 called *A Map Comes to Life*. The film gained some attention, and once she joined the studio full-time, we got our first commission by the Southbank Centre to create twelve short films to promote their classical season 2007–08.

Your animations have a very distinct and characterful style. How did this style develop, and what were your inspirations?
We are both drawn to the surreal, dark, and the mysterious in everyday life. We love craftsmanship, and I think that our style comes naturally.

If your work were a song, what would it be and why?
I think it would have to be a mash-up of

Pottermore
Stills from an animation for Pottermore; an online experience by J. K. Rowling, based around the Harry Potter books.

"We're All Gonna Die" by Scout Niblett, "Work Work" by Bruce Nauman, and "Not Just Anybody" (live version) by Katie Price (a.k.a. Jordan).

As a studio, your work is quite varied, but in recent years, you seem to have been focusing more on your paper animation work. Is this a conscious choice? Would you say that the rise in popularity of papercraft has played a part in this?

The success of *Going West* has probably played a big part in this. We signed up with a great producer, Toby Courlander, who has been successful in getting us a lot of work, which has been challenging and exciting all at the same time. I do feel that there has been increased interest in papercraft in recent years because a lot of creatives are bored sitting in front of a computer all day and would rather use their hands to express themselves.

Your animation Going West has won numerous awards including two Gold Lions at Cannes. How did this project come about, and what kind of planning and preparation goes into an animation like this?

We were commissioned by BBDO in New Zealand to create a stop-frame animation for a viral campaign about the creativity involved in reading. Among a selection of a few different novels, we decided to base it on *Going West* by Maurice Gee, an author from New Zealand. The deadline was set at twelve months from the start of the project, which is unheard of in this industry, but it allowed us time and trust to create an amazing campaign.

We read the book and then researched the novel's scenery in detail (the ferns, the Anglican church, etc.). Then we created a storyboard using a mixture of roughly designed models and drawings with detailed descriptions about the animation, edits, and timings. Once this had been approved by the agency, we

moved on to create and finesse the paper models. We had an oversized *Going West* book bound, in which we made nearly all of the animations. One of the biggest challenges was to design the models so they all fit on the same sheet of paper so the animation seemed to come to life out of the written word on the pages.

Once we reached this stage, we did a few test shoots for timing and focusing purposes before we finally started shooting the final animation. At this point, we barely said anything to each other, with Line concentrating on the animation, and me on the cinematography, focus pulling, and lighting. Shooting the actual film took us about two to three months.

After we shot the final animation, we then discussed the project with our sound designer, who recorded the paper-cutting and folding sounds.

This is where the film finally came to life and became magical.

What challenges did you face on this project?

It was very challenging, but not so much for creative reasons. Rather, because we as a studio made a decision to spend almost an entire year working on the project, without the necessary funding in place to run the studio. By the end of it, we were almost bankrupt. Looking back at it now, it is mad to think that we were in so much debt and that we had to borrow money from friends to go to Cannes to pick up our two Gold Lions.

Looking at your project credits, you seem to be involved in many stages of the creation of your animations, including the photography and directing. How important is it for you

Left and Below
Clouds
Stills from an animation
for Alfred Dunhill
through It's Nice That.

to be this involved in your projects? Is this an approach you have always taken?

We made a decision very early on that we wanted to keep the studio really small, so that we would always be hands-on with our projects. Neither of us is interested in just being art directors directing teams without ever getting our own hands dirty. We love to have the freedom to select the projects we are working on rather than constantly having to take on big commercial projects to pay the staff. The reason for working together in the first place was because we share the same sensibilities and tastes, and we complement each other perfectly with our different skill sets.

Martin, you also tutor at the University of Brighton and Central Saint Martins. How does teaching shape your attitudes toward your own work?

I really enjoy my interaction with the students and always aim to be an inspiration by being ambitious, hard-working, and brutally honest assessing their work. It is a privilege to be a teacher and something that in the U.K. is not appreciated in the same way as it is, for example, in The Netherlands or the United States. I've been teaching almost eleven years, and it has made me more confident about my own work, more analytical, and better at explaining my ideas. I strongly believe that I learn just as much as I'm able to teach the students.

Looking toward the future, what direction do you see your studio going in?

We would definitely like to develop our stop-frame animations and our storytelling skills. We hope to explore different media within stop-frame animation, not just that of paper. We would also like to be ambitious about moving images in general, perhaps more work in live action? In the near future, I hope to have the time to finish my first documentary *The Last Show,* and finally publish my photography book that has been ten years in the making.

Below
On Your Side
Line Andersen hand-cutting pages of a book as part of an animation for Nationwide.

Upside Down House
Kyle created this
hanging house as part
of a project for Lloyds
Bank. Photography by
Sam Hofman.

18

London
UK

Kyle Bean is a freelance illustrator, model-maker, and set designer based in Brighton. He is well known for his conceptual designs, and he has created thought-provoking pieces for international clients such as the BBC, Louis Vuitton, and Selfridges. Kyle graduated from the University of Brighton in 2009 and was the recipient of an ADC Young Guns Award in 2011. Although his work explores a range of materials, he often experiments with paper-cut design.

Kyle Bean

You studied illustration at the University of Brighton. How important do you think this academic training was on your development as an illustrator?
I had a really great time at university, and I think the course was exactly what I needed to help me focus and explore my interests. Before university, I was very torn between pursuing a career in product design and one in a more communication-based design field. The interesting thing about the illustration course at Brighton is that it is very ideas-driven. The materials you use or the format you present your work in is entirely up to the individual. This really worked for me because I could approach the course from a 3-D, tactile perspective, and incorporate my product design interests into my illustration projects. Although I dabbled in creating two-dimensional imagery at university, it was always the 3-D work and animation-based projects that came more naturally to me.

Your work combines model-making and set design. How did you develop this style, and what were your inspirations?
I often find myself in a slightly gray area—somewhere between sculpture, set design, and illustration. Model-making is certainly something I have been doing since a young age, but since university, I have worked within a few different contexts. In fact, my first professional commission was an installation for Liberty, so I learned quickly how to showcase my model-making skills in an environment where I had to consider the interaction between my work, the products, and the passing shoppers. Quite soon afterward, I was being commissioned to produce things in an editorial context. For this, I had to develop my photography skills in order

Paper Suits
A set of paper suits
created for a series of
images showcasing
Louis Vitton accessories.
Photography by Lacey.

to be able to capture the things that I
make in an image. I later realized that
working with still-life photographers
allowed me to create more professional
set designs for commercial clients.

**So what would you say are the benefits
of working with photographers to
shoot your work?**
They can often bring more to the image
than I could myself. I often prefer my
work to be shot in quite a simple and
natural way, but from time to time,
a concept I develop requires a more
experimental approach to the lighting.
I enjoy working with photographers
I know can bring out the best in the
models and sets that I make.

**How does working with a photographer
compare with shooting your own work,
and what effect does it have on the way
you approach a project?**
With smaller editorial pieces that have
a limited budget, I tend to propose
ideas that I know I can shoot myself,
so generally this means, for example,

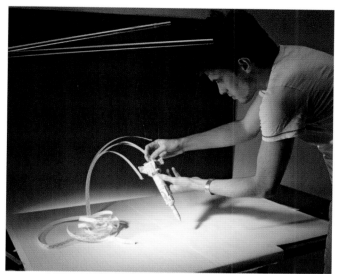

Wall Street Rocket Scientists
Kyle working on an editorial illustration for *Scientific American*. Photography by Owen Silverwood.

keeping to a graphic-based image with simple, soft lighting. However, if the budget allows for it, I can develop ideas that allow for a slightly more complex lighting setup. It also means that I can explore a wider variety of techniques and materials to make the model or set piece. I do enjoy the variety though; I feel as happy working alone as I do collaborating with photographers. I tend to decide which approach I take on a job-by-job basis.

Your work explores a range of different materials, but paper seems to make quite a consistent appearance in your portfolio. When and why did you start using paper in your work, and what is it about the material that attracts you to keep using it?

I enjoy experimenting and learning to work with different materials. Often, the material I use is an integral part of communicating the concept of a particular piece I am creating. Having said that, paper is a material I will always come back to, simply because it is so versatile and able to be transformed in so many ways with relative ease. The fact that paper comes in so many forms means that the results of working with it can seem limitless. And because it is a material that everyone is familiar with, it is inherently relatable; I believe people enjoy seeing how such a humdrum, everyday material can be manipulated so freely. I started playing with the materials in my work at university.

We did not have access to wood or metal workshops, and so I had to find ways of using simple materials around me to create my pieces.

Could you take us through your general working method from the initial briefing stage to the end of the project?

For editorial projects, I often get an article or a brief summary of an article to

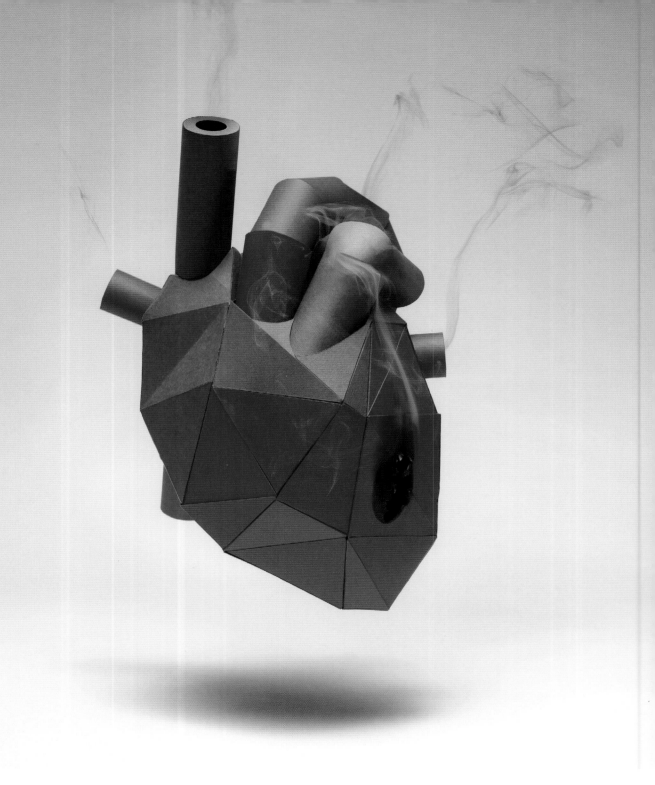

Above
Heart
Kyle created this paper
anatomical heart for
an article about heart
disease in *Men's Health*.
Photography by
Owen Silverwood.

Right
Transformation
Part of a series of five
window displays for
Selfridges inspired
by the law of
conservation of mass:
"Matter cannot be
created or destroyed,
only transformed."
Photography by
Andrew Meredith
and Mike Dodd.

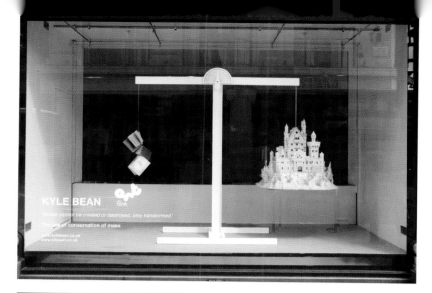

read. After reading and understanding
the story, my approach is then fairly
simple: I try to distill the message
of the article into simple form while
simultaneously considering the
materials that I would use to make the
image. I basically create two lists: (1)
Forms—shape/objects/symbols; (2)
Materials. I choose materials as a way of
highlighting the message of the article.
Once I have the idea for the visual, I
sketch it out and then send the sketch
with a brief description to the client for
feedback. Once approved, I source the
materials and make the physical piece. I
then either photograph the piece myself
or work with a still-life photographer,
depending on the budget and the nature
of the lighting that I want to achieve.

For installation projects, my
approach is similar, but the focus is
very much on the physical pieces that I
am creating and not the photography.
I have to ensure that the models are
made to a very high standard and work
well from all angles when viewed by the
naked eye.

**What would you say have been your
most challenging projects so far?**
The Transformation windows I
produced for Selfridges was a big
challenge in terms of time, scale, and
budget. I was asked to create five
window installations, and once my
concept was approved, I had only three
weeks to make everything and put it all
together for the installation date. What
was brilliant about that project, though,
is that I had free rein to present an idea
that I developed. So despite it being
very challenging, it was one of my most
rewarding commercial projects.

A smaller, but similarly challenging
project I did was for *Men's Health*
magazine. I was commissioned to create
an anatomically correct human heart
out of paper to be photographed for an
article. I had to be quite precise with

Below
Mobile Evolution
A personal project
looking at the evolution
of the mobile phone in
Russian doll form.

my depiction, while at the same time keeping to a geometric, graphic style.

Possibly my most challenging paper-based project was for Peugeot. I designed and art-directed a stop-frame, animated TV commercial; it was a massive learning curve for me. While I had dabbled in animation in the past, I was suddenly having to design my models and sets to be animated in a very slick and professional manner, and work with a big team.

What do you enjoy most about the work you do, and what direction would you like to take it in the future?
The variety of projects is what I really love the most. I enjoy changing between working on small-scale sets and images for magazines to larger-scale

installations and display work. One of my biggest passions aside from design is film. Film is a big part of my life, but it's more of a hobby than something I see as a potential project. I'd love to think that I could do something that combines these interests more though.

Finally, do you have any words of wisdom that you could share with people who are just starting out in this profession?
It's important for you to be happy with the work you are doing, and I think the only way you can do that is by following your gut instincts. Don't be afraid to change things if you are not quite happy. When you are true to yourself and your interests, then good things will happen!

Above
Killing Time
Kyle created this series of realistic paper watches, which when cut into, play with the viewer's perceptions. Photography by Lacey.

26
London
UK

Yulia Brodskaya

Russian born Yulia Brodskaya moved to London in 2004. Her interest in papercraft has seen her develop an incredibly distinctive style that is recognized worldwide. Yulia's modern take on the papercraft practice has since helped her to build an impressive list of clients, including Hermès, Starbucks, Target, Sephora, and the *New York Times* magazine. In 2009, she was named as that year's "breakthrough star" by *Creative Review* magazine.

First, can you tell us a little bit about your background? What brought you to the U.K. from Russia?

I was born in Moscow in 1983 and later moved to the U.K. in 2004 to get a masters in graphic communication at the University of Hertfordshire. During that year, I always felt the "creative vibe" around me, which never happened in Moscow, so I decided to stay and pursue my career here. I started working as a graphic designer and illustrator in 2006, but quickly abandoned computer programs in favor of paper-based art. Soon after discovering my passion and unique style, I was lucky enough to earn an international reputation for my paper artworks. I have calculated recently that I've worked on more than 120 projects over the past five years!

The technique you use is called quilling, which is a very traditional method of papercraft. What led you to start working this way?

I've always had a special fascination with paper. I've tried many different paper-based methods and techniques, such as origami and collage, but the quilling technique turned out to be "the one" for me. I started using it about five years ago when I was creating a self-promotion to send out to potential clients. I was looking for an eye-catching image with my name on the cover. I created a number of hand-drawn variants, but I didn't like any of them, and then I remembered an image from an old schoolbook. It showed paper strips standing on edge, so I tried to make the letters of my name using this technique, and apparently the attempt was successful; over the next couple of months, I switched to paper illustration completely.

Your work is often bold and playful, using bright color palettes against clean white backgrounds. How did you develop this style, and what were your inspirations?

I think it just evolved over time. I started with predominately white paper images, then I tried to use some limited colors. It turned out that the edge-glued color strips against a white background reflect the light in a very interesting way. (The color shadows of the adjacent strips blend and make the whole image richer and visually more interesting.)

If your work were a song, what would it be and why?

Interesting question. I can't name a particular song, but I think it would be something melodic, but not in a sad way—a light "easy-flowing" melody.

Could you briefly take us through your general working method and how you go about planning your artworks?

I always make pencil sketches first and don't start the paper work until the sketches are approved by the client (or until I'm totally happy with the result, if it's a personal work). Sketching is a very important stage because once I've glued a piece of paper, I can't remove it, so

Left
Yulia Brodskaya
working at her desk

Right
Fruit
An illustration
created for
Hennessy.
Photography by
John Ross.

Right
Dairy Milk
An illustration for
Cadbury. Photography
by Michael Leznik.

Loves Doves
Part of a series of self-initiated artworks exploring portraiture and the theme of death in art. Photography by John Ross.

there is no place for errors. I need to have a very clear idea about what I'm doing from the beginning. However, there is always room to experiment when the actual paper work starts because sometimes it is difficult to see what will work best at the outset. Once the paper artwork is ready, it is photographed. This is a very important stage because lighting can make or break this type of paper artwork: It shouldn't be complex, but there are certain "no-nos" when it comes to photography.

What tools do you use to create your work? Are there any particular paper stocks that you favor?
I use a cocktail straw and little cocktail sticks for rolling the paper strips. (I didn't know that there are specially designed tools available when I taught myself to shape the paper strips.) I use lots of different types of paper, but in general, I prefer heavy ones that are still flexible enough to be rolled without creasing or exfoliating.

You've recently been developing a range of personal works that take a more artistic approach focusing around portraiture. What was your inspiration for this series?
I'm happy to get as many commissions as I do, but after a while, I started to think that I was missing something, so that's why I decided to dedicate some of my time to personal work. I've chosen to work with portraiture because I'm always curious to find out what can and cannot be said within the boundaries of a chosen medium and material—if it is possible to successfully convey meaning and emotions. And what is more challenging than a person's face?

Far Left
Gypsy
Personal project.
Photography by
John Ross.

Left
Babushka
Personal project.
Photography by
John Ross.

Very true! Most of the characters in your personal portraits are based on elderly people. What led you to choose these particular characters to illustrate?

There are two main reasons, I think. One is related to the theme of death in art; there are hundreds and hundreds of works of art devoted to the subject. My personal interest is in the aspect of approaching death—old age. I'm fascinated by it; it worries me. I have really strong, mixed feelings about it that make me look through photographs of old people in a search for inspiration for my personal work. Another reason is material- and technique-related: The edge-glued paper strips are a great way of depicting the wrinkles. For a younger face, I would probably look for a slightly different paper treatment, but I'm definitely going to attempt that at some point too.

What would you say have been your most challenging projects so far?

In general, I enjoy projects most when I'm given creative freedom to follow my own vision and direction; the more rigid and controlling the client, the more stressful any cooperation becomes, and often the result is not as good as when I am given more freedom and control. I suppose this is a common thing among designers and artists.

Looking toward the future, in what direction would you like to take your work?

I would like to explore the fine-art direction a bit more, and maybe look into mass production. Also animation. I have many different plans. I'm sure that the most exciting project in my career is yet to come.

Double Prism
Part of a set of personal artworks created by Bianca titled *Form in White*. Photography by Jacob Ring.

Bianca Chang

Bianca Chang is a designer and artist based in Sydney, Australia. Her works explore geometric forms using a very unique style of layering multiple sheets of consumer waste recycled paper.

Can you tell us a little bit about yourself and your background?
I started tertiary studies in law, visual communication, and audio engineering before realizing that what I wanted to do was much more multi-dimensional and undefined than what was offered. As a result, I dropped out of university, started working, and taught myself what I needed to learn along the way. I've worked as a graphic designer for the past four years—first in Singapore, now in Sydney. I currently work part-time for the prominent Australian designer Mark Gowing. He is a generous mentor and friend. During this time, I was encouraged to develop my work with paper sculpture.

Your work crosses the boundaries of both illustration and fine art. How did you develop this style, and what were your inspirations?
The style is an extension of my design practice. Whether they're typographic, abstracted, or geometric, I approach the forms I create in the same way I would approach a design project — using principles such as employing a grid to make decisions about compositional layout.

Minimalism seems to play an important part in your work and the way you present yourself online: Your choice of paper stock is generally quite simple, and there aren't many details about you on your website. Is this a conscious choice?
It is and it isn't. I think minimalism in the works themselves is a result of experimentation. The compositions become stronger visually when there aren't too many elements. It is also less time-consuming to complete the cutting of a minimal design. I choose simple stocks so that nothing distracts the viewer from the strength of the form. As for my website, I made the conscious decision to remove information about myself because I don't think it affects whether a stranger likes my work or not, especially on the Internet. I don't make a living on commercial commissions, nor do I wish to. Galleries and curators receive information about me in person.

Your work is amazingly precise and often involves very clever uses of layering and depth. How much planning is involved in creating these artworks?
There is quite a bit of planning involved.

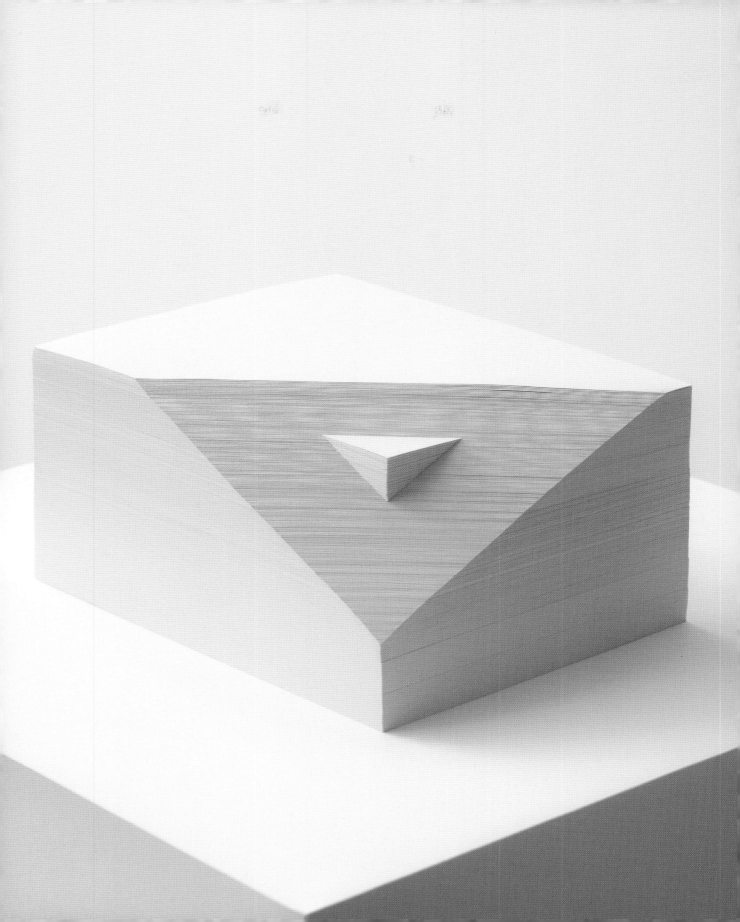

I can't really change my mind about something halfway through cutting, so everything is set in concrete before I start. The only mocking up I do is a 2-D top-view in Adobe Illustrator to make sure the measurements I've chosen work out. Doing this digitally makes it easier to chop and change. From this map, I can also figure out how many sheets will be needed and what depth the finished piece will have. Then in terms of plotting and cutting, I do that all by hand.

Once your mock-ups are complete, how do you go about creating your artworks?

I'll print out the design and leave it out for a week or two to make sure it's what I want to create. I then cut a ream of paper to size, plot out the design on each sheet, and start hand-cutting, layer by layer, from the bottom of the piece to the top. For these pieces, I favor uncoated paper stocks that are wood-free, acid-free, and off white.

Above
Twin
A personal artwork combining Bianca's layered paper-cut style with typography. Photography by Jacob Ring.

Right
Anatomic Eye
Part of a series of artworks created for OPSM Opticians. Photography by Jacob Ring.

Next page. Clockwise from top left
Bianca working at her desk. *Noise II*, *Head I* and *Gradient*. All personal artworks photographed by Jacob Ring.

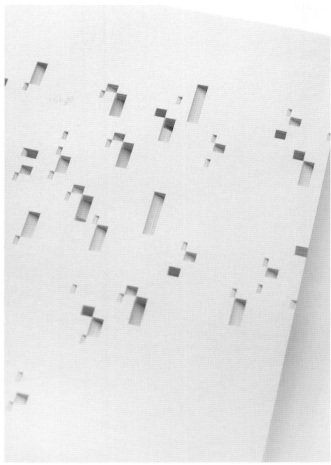
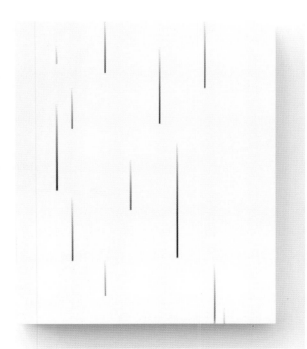

Rotation IV
Part of a set of personal artworks created by Bianca titled *Form in White*. Photography by Jacob Ring.

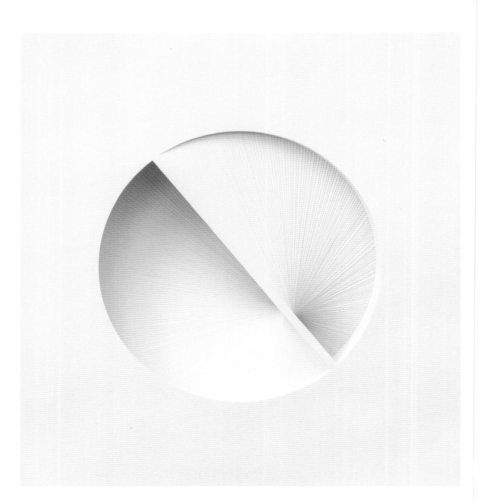

How do you manage your time, and what tricks have you discovered along the way to help you speed up the process?

I think repetition has honed my cutting skills. Each piece seems to take less and less time, because I make fewer mistakes, and I'm more accurate than I was a few years ago. I think I've also become a better decision maker, which saves a lot of time.

What would you say have been your most challenging projects so far?

The most challenging projects are ones with open briefs. Commercial commissions are relatively challenge-free because there are a set of parameters that must be met. The problem solving is in the logistics, which has a definite process and outcome. When I create works for exhibition, I find it much more challenging because there are no restrictions.

Looking toward the future, what direction do you see your work going in?

I don't know what form my work will take in a few years' time. I'm just happy to take the opportunities that present themselves as they come. I see my work in paper as something that will complement my other creative pursuits quite nicely. I am very passionate about making ceramics and hope to devote more time to pottery in the future. I am also helping my husband develop his photographic services business. So who knows?

Finally, do you have any words of wisdom that you could share with people who are just starting out in this profession?

Perseverance is key—nothing happens overnight.

Rinascente
Part of a series of
window displays created
for Palermo.

40

Paris
France

Le Creative Sweatshop

Le Creative Sweatshop (a.k.a. Julien Morin, Stéphane Perrier, and Matthieu Missiaen) is a creative studio based in Paris working in the fields of fashion, design, contemporary art, and architecture. The studio is committed to originality and quality, and their hand-crafted design approach, which comprises fixed and dynamic 3-D work, has a unique identity, leading to a range of commissions for the likes of Nissan, Stella McCartney, and *Bombek* magazine.

Stéphane, your work explores a range of different materials, but paper seems to make quite a consistent appearance in your portfolio. What led you to start using paper in your work?
Paper was the beginning of our work. It was the first material that we used and one we still use from time to time. We keep using it because there are a lot of ways to work with paper—you can work with it in 3-D, layer it, mold it, and manipulate it in many other ways.

Your work has quite a sleek and stylish feel. How did this style develop, and what were your inspirations?
For three years now, we've been working with all kinds of materials, and our goal has always been to combine those new materials in order to find new textures and ways to astonish people with something that they'd never normally see. That's why we've worked with concrete, jelly, paper, plaster, and other substances. Our inspirations, like everybody else's, are a combination of what we see in magazines, on blogs, and at art exhibitions. We try new things every day, and post new images on our blog to keep our ideas fresh.

Left
Rinascente
Part of a series of
window displays created
for Palermo.

Right
Hermès
LCSS created this series
of paper objects as part
of a window display
for Hermès flagship
store in Shaghai, China.
Production by The
Imaginers.

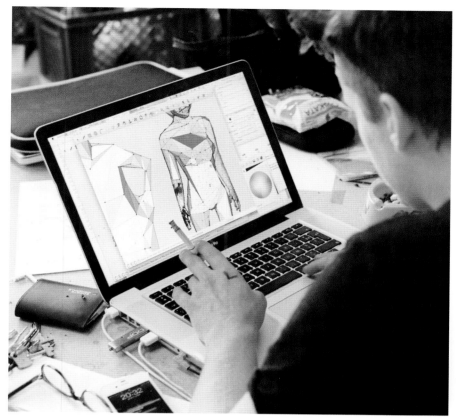

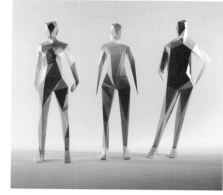

What's the current design scene like in Paris? Is paper a popular design and image-making tool?

The Paris design scene involves a mix of illustration, 3-D renderings, and classic photography. We work more in the abstract, and try to keep our images stunning and weird. Paper tends to be used less in image-making. Even we don't use it very often; we often opt for other materials to work with.

You have a large circle of creatives that you work with on projects. What do you see as the benefit of collaborating with others?

Collaboration with other creatives is always a good thing—it forces us to see what's going on from another point of view. Someone who's not from our studio brings new ways to view a project. We sometimes collaborate with photographers. Some of them have really enhanced the final project.

What would you say have been your most challenging projects so far?

Our work for La Rinascente in Palermo was probably our most challenging project to date because of the

Think Outside the Parking Box
An advertising campaign for Nissan. Photography by Grégoire Alexandre.

organization, the number of window displays, the location in the south of Italy, and the short time between the beginning and the end of the job. It was really hard to realize a project like that because it came at a time when the studio had just been put together, and we were not as experienced as we are today. It was ultimately a really good project though.

How do you manage your time, and what tricks have you discovered along the way to help you speed up the process?
Time is a very important factor in our work. The timescales we're given allow us to do some projects, but we have to refuse others because of a lack of time. We don't have any particular tricks to speed things up—there are three of us working within LCSS, and everyone will have something to do. Sometimes we do use software to speed up the process, but the final rendering is always made in 3-D, so the process remains fairly long.

Looking toward the future, what direction do you see your studio going in?
You can never say, but if we could make a wish, we'd hope that our studio will still be working on many different projects that push us forward. Perhaps to work on more renderings at the crossroads of set design, new technologies, and photography.

Finally, do you have any words of wisdom that you could share with people who are just starting out in this profession?
Work a lot! Make something new every day, even if you don't like it. Experiment, and ideas will come. That's how we roll!

QASHQAI
URBANPROOF

PAR LE CREATIVE SWEATSHOP
À suivre, le concours Designboom de Nissan « Think outside the parking box * »

www.nissan.fr

URBANPROOF : À l'épreuve de la ville. HARD CORE LEVEL 6 : Niveau final 6. *Stationnement d'idées interdit. Modèle présenté :
Nissan QASHQAI Tekna 1.5 dCi 106 ch avec option peinture métallisée (vitres avant surteintées présentées non disponibles en France).
Consommations (l/100km) : urbaine : 6.0, extra-urbaine : 4.8, mixte : 5.2. Emissions CO_2 (g/km) : 139. NISSAN WEST EUROPE SAS
au capital de 4 253 835 €, RCS Versailles 699 809 174 - Parc de Pissaloup - 13, avenue Jean d'Alembert - 78194 Trappes Cedex.

Elise is a London-based artist and photographer. She studied fine art at Chelsea School of Art and works on both personal and commissioned projects from her studio in Borough. Elise's practice combines photography with sculpture to explore the constructed image. Her photographs of large-scale installations blend two and three dimensions to form hyperreal spaces, captured by the photographic lens. Recent commissions have been for *British Vogue*, Ford, Nokia, Sony PlayStation, and Virgin.

Elise

Unlike the other artists in this book, you label yourself as a photographer rather than a set designer, but your work explores both realms. Where do you draw the line between the two?
I don't draw the line between the two. Both of these processes are essential to making the final image. Whether I'm drawing or constructing the elements, building the set, lighting the installation, or capturing the photograph, each of these detailed processes is equally important. Also, as I build the installation from the position of the camera lens, the set and photography are closely linked. The perspective of the camera lens dictates the overall form and coherence of the composition.

On a conceptual level, the process of transforming the three-dimensional set into the flat, 2-D space of the photograph begins to question dimension, scale, and perspective. There's a really interesting visual tension between these different aspects of image-making.

You seem to enjoy taking charge of the whole image-making process. Do you ever collaborate on projects with other set designers and photographers?
I've always worked on every aspect of the image-making process myself, from drawing and building, to shooting the final image. I really enjoy each aspect of the process, so I prefer it this way. When I was at art school, we were given a studio, some great tutors, and the freedom to create. I think this was an excellent induction into making art. I really like the coherence of concept and style this creative independence allows.

Your work explores the relationships of objects and textures from everyday life, using bright, bold color palettes. How did this style develop, and what were your inspirations?
I'm very much a "pop artist" in the materials, colors, and objects I use in my images: the plastic surface of everyday objects and pound shop kitsch. The use of these materials has always been at the core of my practice, and I've always been really inspired by the stuff we consider banal or unimportant, as well as the rubbish that ends up in the bin. There's something strangely humorous when these objects are represented in a way that gives them visual significance. This sense of humor and familiarity adds another dimension to the work, where throwaway objects jostle absurdly for

Elise working in her studio on the *Tetrahedron* series.

visual importance. I'm also interested in the language of color, and in the way different colors communicate to us on both a visceral and emotional level, as well as through a more complex, cultural set of values.

The inspirations for my work vary from one image to the next. For a photograph I've been working on recently, I've been looking at the sculptor and artist Eduardo Paolozzi. For another new series, I've been particularly influenced by the colors and playfulness of the Memphis Group design collective. I also find that the materials and objects I use shape the work I'm making. Whether it's paper, polystyrene, plastic, or found objects, these materials offer all sorts of creative possibilities.

Although you often use a range of different materials, paper seems to make quite a consistent appearance throughout your portfolio. What led you to start using paper in your work, and what is it about the material that attracts you to keep using it?
Paper has always been really important. It's an incredibly flexible material, in that it can be used both two and three dimensionally. It's lightweight, extremely versatile, and pliable. It offers endless surfaces and textures to work with. Also, as drawing is so integral to what I do, paper allows me to print, draw, paint, or construct anything I need, so it really is an invaluable material in my work. I can't remember a time when I didn't use it.

Could you briefly take us through your general working method?
I always begin with an initial drawing of the installation I'm going to create. This drawing enables me to work out the composition, as well as important questions of scale, material, lighting and so on. Often, this will be a simple line drawing, but sometimes, particularly for commissions, I'll create a Photoshop rendition of the final image, showing

exact color, light, and shadows. This acts as a visual guide for me to build the installation exactly as drawn. So drawing really is at the core of the process.

In terms of the set, I may have specific, sourced objects in mind. I may also be making and printing various elements. These will depend on the initial drawing, in which I'll also work out all sizing and specifics. There's inevitably a lot of printing, cutting, and construction at this stage of the project. I make sure I have every element made, sourced, and supplied before I start the next stage of building the set. At this point, I'll set up the camera, as I create the installation from the position of the lens. I work between camera and set as I build, making sure the image coheres with the drawing I've created beforehand. The methods of set building vary, depending on the installation, and will involve all sorts of techniques including suspending, gluing and constructing, using rods, clamps, wire and so on.

I spend a lot of time carefully lighting the installation, because it is so important to the success of the final image. I shoot tethered, straight into my Mac because it gives me a lot of control of the photographic process. The image then ends up back on the computer. I do all my own postproduction because I like to keep my work as naturalistic and real as I can. This is important to me, because I want the materials and lighting, rather than the postproduction, to dictate the style of the final image.

What tools do you use to create your work? Are there any particular paper stocks that you favor?
My studio is full of paper, acrylic sheets, polystyrene, lighting stands, paint tins, and endless boxes of unusual objects I've sourced over the years. My Mac, camera, and lighting are also central to my working process. All of my images begin and end on the computer, from

Clockwise from Top Left

Leaves Series
A set made out of bubblegum and both paper and real leaves.

Leaves Series
Elise cutting out the leaves ready to be added to the set.

MW
Commission for McCann Worldgroup.

City Cartoon
Part of a series of sets created for Nokia.

planning and drawing the elements to postproduction. And because I shoot tethered, the process of capturing the image is also digital. I feel fortunate to have grown as an artist alongside the development of digital technology. This has been invaluable, because it has really enhanced my practice.

Paper is also important, and I use it both as a material and as a practical tool. I print the drawn elements for my installations on all sorts of different paper stocks. The variety of finishes and textures makes it incredibly versatile to work with. Different stocks give very different visual effects and play a role in the mood or style of the final image. I also work with laser-cutting processes. There's an interesting difference between objects that are handcrafted and the machine cut, digitally drawn, or mass-produced. I create handmade sculptures, yet at

the same time, I also use a computer and machine processes.

Working as both the set designer and photographer as you do must be very time-consuming. How do you manage your time, and what tricks have you discovered along the way to help you speed up the process?
Each image throws up new challenges, and in a way, I quite like making things hard for myself—that's part of developing as an artist. There are many tried-and-tested methods that you learn along the way, but I'm always keen to experiment with new techniques, materials, and setups that enable me to push my ideas further. But returning to a point I made earlier, I think that planning is essential in creating the sort of work I make. Producing a preliminary, scale-accurate drawing helps me to build exactly what I have in mind,

and it's a great deal easier resolving compositional issues in a drawing than in the build process. So this definitely makes things more time efficient.

What would you say have been your most challenging projects so far?
Every project is challenging in its own way because there are always different demands on the image-making process, whatever the project's material or scale. With every new project, it feels as though I'm on a unique journey. I think the new discoveries along the way keep the work fresh and interesting. I've recently completed a commission for Ford, for example, where I was given just twenty-four hours to create a giant installation of paper and polystyrene objects, with a Ford Fiesta suspended in the middle. I particularly love working on a big scale like this, because the experience of the installation

Diamond
Work in progress shots
and final image for
one of Elise's personal
projects.

becomes completely immersive and all-encompassing.

Looking toward the future, what direction would you like to take your work?

I'm making ever-larger installations, and so scale is really the focus for me, going forward. I'm also producing ever-larger photographic prints, and I'm interested in how these prints, because of their size, start to become impressive installations in themselves. I'm just about to make a really enormous image, made up of panels, each one comprising a different area of a photographed installation, and which together form a gigantic picture. Hundreds of objects cascade downward in the image called *Plastic Waterfall*. I'm inspired by how, historically in painting, panel pictures have been used to represent highly complex visual stories.

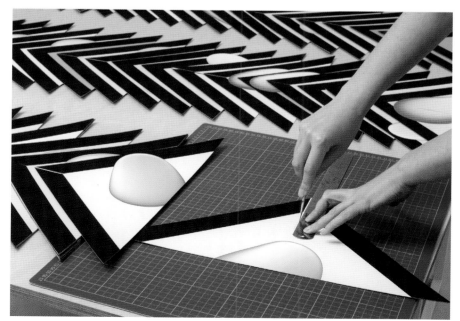

The 24 Hour Fiesta Project
Asked to create a campaign to showcase the new Ford Fiesta, Elise created a giant installation where she suspended the car with hundreds of familiar objects.

Micro Architecture
A personal project
exploring Micro-
Architecture in various
forms. Photography by
Tom Joye.

54
Brussels
Belgium

Alexis Facca is a set designer who grew up in Toulouse in the southwest of France, "where the sun shines and where we cook France's best food," he tells me. He now lives and works in Brussels and has built up an impressive portfolio, which explores a range of different materials and techniques.

What led you to start using paper in your work, and what is it about this material that attracts you to keep using it?

I started studying interior design, but university was so boring and so slow, so I quit and took a job at a printing house. While working there, I discovered lots of different types of paper, so I started to experiment with it, creating shapes with paper and then posting the results on Facebook. Friends asked me to create flyers and posters for their music acts, and one day a creative agency contacted me for my first "real" papercraft job. A few months later, I left the printing house.

Your miniature set designs have an air of Thomas Demand about them, although on a much smaller scale. How did you develop this way of working? Would you list Demand among your inspirations?

I codeveloped a project with the photographer Tom Joye, with whom I share a studio. I don't really remember how the idea came to us, but we both love furniture and interior design—it wouldn't surprise me if the project emerged from the pages of *Wallpaper** magazine. We hadn't heard of Thomas Demand before the project, and we both discovered his fabulous work while working on it. I really like and respect his work, which is totally crazy, because it's all life-size!

Could you briefly take us through your general working method? What tools do you use to create your work?

When I receive a brief, I'll imagine the size and the arrangement in my head. Sometimes I try to draw it, but that's not always easy because the forms can be complex, and I'm pretty bad at drawing! If a client does ask, I'll try to draw it. I say "try" because a seven-year-old draws better than I do. Then I'll draw the patterns on paper and try to build the piece. If I'm not satisfied, I rework the pattern.

To create the work, I use a scalpel, a set square and rulers, a cutter, glue and tape, and a compass—nothing original. I do have some favorite paper stocks, but it depends on the project. Most of the time, I prefer plain colors without texture; I hate Mi-teintes paper. But for my project, *The Office*, I used some very realistic textures for wood, leather, stone and so on. This was probably one

Alexis Facca

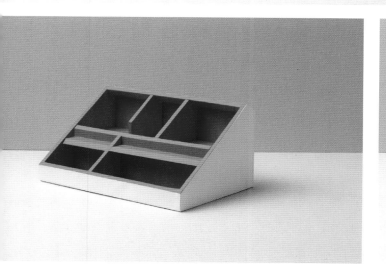

of my more challenging projects due to the tiny details and precision involved.

What tricks have you discovered along the way to help you speed up the process?

I've tried using lot of things: a laser cutter, or a computer-assisted cutting blade—but the results have always been disappointing. I think the best thing that I've found during the past couple of years is transparent double-sided tape. It's honestly changed the way I work.

You are obviously someone who likes to keep yourself busy. Alongside your set design work, you also run the design studio Holy Soakers and the music blog Hors d'œuvres. How do you manage your time, and what drives you as a creative?

I give much of my time to music. With my friend Romain, I set up Holy Soakers, a PR/graphic design agency that promotes emerging bands. We've also created Hors d'œuvres, an online mixtape repository where we ask musical artists to answer the question: "What are your influences?" We give them a sonic carte blanche, their only challenge being to answer the question differently. And all these mixtapes are downloadable for free. I don't really manage my time; I try to give my best to all my projects.

Finally, what words of advice would you give to people who are just starting out in this business?

No matter what you do, there will always be people who'll hate you, and people who'll love you and your work. So, my advice? Just do what you want, what you love, and have fun.

Above
Solvéo
Still from a stop-frame animation for Solvéo Energies to promote their implantation in the Landes region.

CITROËN ⌃ GSA

Y659 WEG

GSA X3
A personal project
paying homage to
the Citroën GSA X3.
Photography by
Tom Joye.

Y659 WEG

The Office
A personal project
exploring office
spaces. This series of
paper-craft scenes was
created to resemble
80s advertising.
Photography by
Tom Joye.

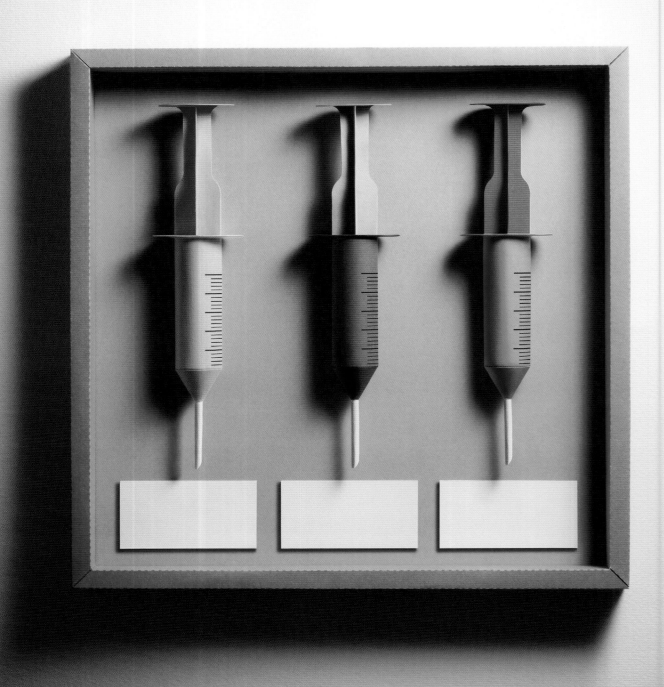

Proto Magazine
Part of a series of models for Proto Magazine's article on prescription drug shortages in the US. Photography by Chris Turner.

Helen Friel

Paper engineer and illustrator Helen Friel graduated from Central Saint Martins in 2009 with a B.A. in graphic design. She now works in London and has created an eclectic range of pieces for clients including Harrods, *Vogue*, and *Fast Company* magazine. Helen's work combines elements of paper-cut, model-making, and collage and has been featured in a number of leading publications including *Grafik*, *Design*Sponge* online, and *Aesthetica* magazine.

You studied graphic design at Central Saint Martins but now work predominantly as an illustrator. Why the transition? Does your training in graphic design play a part in the way you work now?

The first year of the graphic design degree at CSM gives you a chance to try everything. I was very tempted to pursue typography, but in my second year, I decided to specialize in illustration; it gave me more options to develop my own images. Although the result of my work is now illustration, I think I approach projects from a graphic-design perspective. I love nets and grid systems!

What led you to start using paper in your work, and what is it about the material that attracts you to keep using it?

I loved pop-up books when I was little, and when I was at university, the paper trend was just starting. People like Rob Ryan were becoming better known, and I was drawn to the precision that's involved in paper engineering. I'm not very good with the hit-and-miss nature of painting and drawing, whereas with paper, you can keep evolving the work until it's exactly as you want it. While I was studying, I did a couple of projects using paper, which went well. It followed from there.

Could you briefly take us through your general working method?

Once I've nailed down the concept with the client, I go away and create a sketch of the final image. This is crucial because once a set is made, photographed, and retouched, it's tricky to make changes. The next stage is designing the nets for the models, which is done in Adobe Illustrator. I don't usually make prototypes, because it's time-consuming, and deadlines are often short, but by cutting pieces on a plotter, any mistakes are pretty easy to

rectify. The models are all put together using a glue syringe and UHU glue—it's the most precise method I've found and creates a very strong bond. Then the sets are photographed. If they need to appear to float, they're wired up, and the wires are retouched out.

What tools do you use to create your work? Are there any particular paper stocks that you favor?
To cut the work, I use a combination of scalpels and a plotter. I always have on hand: metal rulers, glue syringes, UHU, a print roller, a bradle, and magic tape. My favorite paper stock is GF Smith's Colorplan. It comes in a beautiful range of colors and is great to work with.

You've worked with a number of photographers to shoot your sets. How important is collaboration in your working practice?
Incredibly important; collaborations

have pushed and developed my work. I first worked with Chris Turner two years ago, and he's photographed most of my work since. We've worked on a lot of personal projects together, and it's great to have two perspectives on things.

The most ambitious project we've undertaken was a 90-second stop-frame animation, called *Revolution*. Jess Deacon also collaborated with us as the animator on the project, and it was something that none of us could have produced alone. I think collaboration is vital to keep your work fresh—it means you can create something that is more than the sum of its parts.

You also sometimes photograph your illustrations yourself. How does working with a photographer compare with shooting your own work, and what effect does it have on the way you approach a project?

If a project is pretty straightforward, I can usually shoot it myself. I have a small studio setup and a good camera—although, if time and budget allow, I always try to encourage clients to use an independent photographer. I think having an objective pair of eyes enhances the work.

You recently won a SPD merit award for your work for Proto magazine about prescription drug shortages in the United States. How did this project come about, and what was your thought process behind it?
It was a really interesting project and another in collaboration with Chris Turner. Proto gave me the article and some rough ideas of what they'd like, but I was given a lot of creative freedom. The idea was very simple— that shortages were so dire that drugs would soon only be seen in a museum. I created bright models, and Chris

Left page
Still Life on Earth
Part of a series of three set designs for *Vanity Fair*'s jewelery feature. Photography by Chris Turner

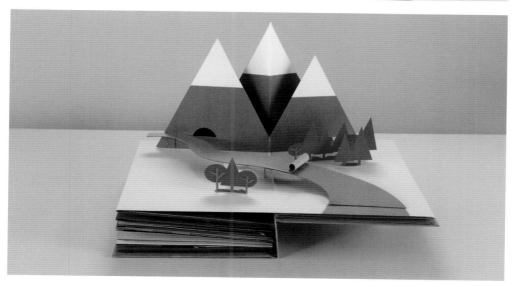

This page
Revolution
Stills from a stop-frame animation created in collaboration with Jess Deacon and Chris Turner depicting the journey of a single water droplet.

Right
Helen at her desk.

Below
Predictions
Part of a series of
artworks exploring the
art of hepatomancy—
predicting the future by
studying animal entrails.
Photography by Chris
Turner.

shot them with a dark feel—the visual
shorthand of valuable and rare items
seemed to work well.

How do you manage your time, and what tricks have you discovered along the way to help you speed up the process?

The turnaround for editorial
illustrations is often very short, so I
have to be realistic about what can be
achieved in the time even before I start
sketching. Illustrator is a brilliant tool
for quick and accurate nets, and I can
output these straight to the plotter.
This means that if something needs
changing, I can recut it quickly. I make a
lot of lists while I'm working and keep to
my calendar religiously to see how long
things take.

What would you say have been your most challenging projects so far?

Generally, the wider the brief, the
more difficult I find the project. For
Predictions, a personal project, there
wasn't really a starting point, and I
struggled for weeks to set myself some
limits. I spent a lot of time trawling
around the Internet before I stumbled
across an article about hepatomancy, the
art of divining the future from animal
entrails, which gave me the idea.

Finally, do you have any words of wisdom that you could share with people who are just starting out in this profession?

If you're still studying, do as much "real-
life" work as possible before you leave;
it'll give you a head start if your work
is already around when you graduate.
Make sure you have a well-designed
website, and promote yourself: Send
work to blogs and talk to people. Also,
bounce ideas off others—they might see
an angle that you can't. I'm still learning
this myself—I like to work alone, but
having a fresh perspective on a problem
really helps.

Get Lost
Cover and feature
illustrations for
Ryanair's *Let's
Go* magazine.
Photography by
Jessica Flavin.

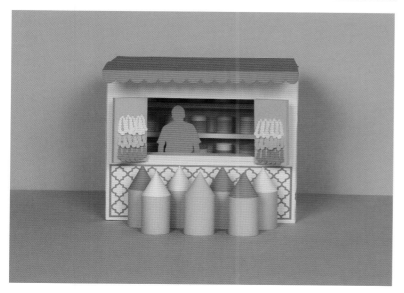

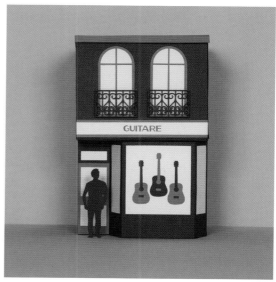

Helen Friel 65

Hort.ex #04
A personal project
combining paper
cuttings with collaged
magazine imagery.

66

New York

USA

Mayuko Fujino

Mayuko Fujino is a paper-cut artist from Tokyo, currently based in New York City. Her work explores a unique style of paper-cutting, combining paper-cut stencils inspired by *katazome*—a traditional Japanese stencil-cutting technique—layered on top of bold collages sourced from the pages of magazines.

What led you to start using paper in your work?

In 1999, I happened to watch a video in a museum, which introduced Keisuke Serizawa's working process. He was a textile designer known for his katazome work, a Japanese traditional stencil-dyeing method in which handmade paper is used to create the stencils. I was fascinated by the cutting process, because it looked so fun, and somehow, I was sure that I could do it too. So I started doing it. The touch and feel of paper and its lightness have simply given me great joy since then.

You have quite a unique style, combining paper-cuttings layered on top of collage. How did this style develop?

One day, I was looking at a catalog of carpet designs, which had sample images cut out into the shapes of birds, leaves, and fruits. That gave me the idea of putting different textures underneath a paper cutout. I tried several materials such as beads, threads, bits of metal, and bark. I still think there are many other materials I can explore, but for now, I find the pages of magazines the most interesting to use. Magazines are like miniatures of human society, and their images both affect and reflect how we see things. Using them for collage feels somewhat violent because it fragments those public images. But I also see the technique as humorous—like with doodles on school books, any important historical figure stops being a hero and becomes a monster as soon as he gets a few brushstrokes on his face; it is an act of disassembling a context and creating another one. I enjoy playing with all these feelings when making a collage. I love seeing all those bits of pages and destroyed contexts, put together with paper cutouts, obtain a new life as a beautiful cluster of colors and textures.

If your work were a song, what would it be and why?

The song of a mourning dove mixed with a train horn and sounds of traffic in my neighborhood—a simple repeated melody interrupted by another context with noises in the background. That's the kind of relationship I'm trying to create between my paper cutouts and collage.

Where do you get your inspiration for your paper-cut artworks?

The initial idea sprouts when something strikes me, and my working process is to

figure out what it means to me and where it is heading. For example, I created a series of pieces featuring anteaters exploring an alien planet—that idea was sparked when I visited a zoo and saw an anteater there. I used to work at the zoo, so I'd seen the animal a couple of times, but I was never particularly drawn to it; somehow that day it inspired me. I went home and made the first image of an anteater being abducted by a UFO. Then one by one, sort of like pieces of a jigsaw puzzle, other scenes came to me. I worked on the anteater images for three years and eventually realized that the work was an allegory for violence and sexuality and an attempt to resolve the conflict between rejection and acceptance, while simultaneously suggesting a route toward happiness. It was also a therapeutic process for me, a reenactment of difficult experiences in my life set in an imaginary world. Each of my series has a unique goal; each one feels completed when it is understood.

Where do you source your collage material? Is the content important, or are you looking more for textural elements?
I like old magazines found in junk stores and online, or ones given to me by acquaintances. I generally look for textural elements and colors. I usually start with one little piece and then find another to follow it, trying to find a natural connection between them and then see where the piece goes.

What would you say have been your most challenging projects so far?
I worked on a project called I *FOUND YOU* in 2011, which was a series of artworks using portrait photos of seventy-one strangers and friends. It was part of an art festival called UAMO, which took place in Munich. I worked on the project with Los Angeles–based artist Jonny Coleman. I don't usually collaborate on my projects, so that was

a bit hard. But it was a good learning experience for me.

Looking toward the future, where do you see your work going?
Besides improving and expanding my current paper-cut work, I am interested in doing projects in public spaces. I have just finished my first-ever window installation at a bookstore in Brooklyn called *Desert Island*. It was a new experience for me, not only because it was my first time involving three-dimensional work, but also because it felt like a very different way to relate to those viewing my work. People on the street were having fun looking at it while I was installing it. I imagine that it could be a similar feeling to when musicians do live shows instead of studio recordings. I'd like to experience those kinds of interactions with viewers more, so I am hoping to work on more outdoor projects, such as murals or public beautification programs.

Above
Birthday Party
Personal project.

Left
Hort.ex #02
Work in progress photo
and final illustration
of one of Mayuko's
personal projects.

Water
Part of a series of self-initiated artworks titled *Kings & Warriors.*

Higan Shigan
Part of a series of self-
initiated artworks titled
Kings & Warriors.

Horrorgami
Marc created this
series of kirigami sets
inspired by infamous
haunted buildings.

Marc Hagan-Guirey

Marc Hagan-Guirey, also known as Paper Dandy, is a British designer and artist specializing in the Japanese art form kirigami. He burst onto the scene in 2012 with his groundbreaking debut show Horrorgami, which featured thirteen original kirigami buildings based on infamous haunted locations from cult movies. The exhibition received international acclaim, and was featured on *ABC News*, *Wired*, *GQ*, and *Time Out* to name but a few.

You only recently started working with paper, having built up a career as a senior creative designer and digital art director. Why the transition? Why paper?
It was all a bit of an accident. Up until April 2012, I was head of design for a boutique advertising agency. I'd been with them for three and a half years, and if I'm honest, I was getting itchy feet. I've always been hugely interested in architecture and property, so when an opportunity arose to invest in a large derelict building with a friend—an experienced property developer—I

leaped at the chance. My colleague was going to be the main financier, and I was going to manage the project as well as create and design the space. My notice period was three months, but to get a head start, I began working on a scheme for the building in the evenings and on weekends. It was a Grand Designs in the making, but on my final day at work, we had to pull out of the sale because of various planning issues. Essentially, I became jobless. Being quite a cautious person, I've always been prepared for such events and decided to take a couple of months off

Left
Marc working at his studio.

Right
The Overlook Hotel
A kirigami set inspired by the hotel featured in *The Shining*.

Below
112 Ocean Avenue
A kirigami set inspired by the *Amityville Horror*.

to think what my next move was going to be. That's when kirigami became my focus. So although I left advertising to make a real house, I ended up making paper houses.

The technique you use is called kirigami, which is a traditional Japanese art form, using a single sheet of cut paper to create the artwork. What led you to start working this way, and what were your inspirations?
I started experimenting with kirigami in October 2009. When I visited Los Angeles in 2010, a friend and my partner had gone to the trouble to arrange for me to be shown around one of my favorite buildings of all time: Frank Lloyd Wright's 1923 Ennis House. It's one of Wright's greatest masterpieces—you'd recognize it as the exterior of Deckard's apartment in *Blade Runner*. It's also the exterior to the mansion in the Vincent Price horror, *House on Haunted Hill*. Due to unfortunate choices in building materials, it's long been in a state of disrepair, and in 1993, a hugely damaging earthquake left it

barely clinging to the hill upon which it was built. The charity trying to restore it had run out of money and was forced to put it on the market for something like $15 million. Having been out of bounds to the public for some 20 years, the scheming duo seized the opportunity to get me through the door. I was blissfully unaware until we pulled up outside its gates. Posing as British gentry interested in purchasing the property, we walked around asking the usual mundane questions about the plumbing and the electrics, while on the inside, I was terrified of being rumbled. Once I had relaxed, it was actually the closest thing I've ever had to a spiritual experience—you could say it was life-changing. Returning to the U.K., I wanted to make something to commemorate the experience, and I set my mind to making a model of some kind as a gift for them both. That's when I came across kirigami.

You recently created a series of sets based on infamous haunted buildings cleverly titled Horrorgami. How did

this series come about, and why did you pick this particular theme?

There are so many existing kirigami replicas of buildings such as St Paul's Cathedral in London, or the Empire State Building in New York, that I really found that area of the art form a bit boring. I'm a huge *Addams Family* fan, and since seeing it as a kid, I've been rather obsessed with the mansion from the 1993 film. It was pretty clear that's what my next subject would be. Through a bit of online snooping, I managed to get hold of the email address of the chap who designed the house: Laurence (Larry) Hubbs. I wrote him an email, attaching some photos of the kirigami model, and a few weeks later, he replied saying how much he loved it. He then sent me super-size scans of his original plans and elevation drawings. I was actually quite tearful. By creating that building, he'd genuinely become one of my childhood heroes. Needless to say, I sent the model to him.

I've always been a huge horror film fan, and it suddenly struck me one day

that, coincidentally, I had made two "haunted" movie houses. Once I realized that, my obsession with horror movies had a new creative outlet, and I set about making more. Thirteen models seemed like a fitting number to work toward. I made a couple more and then took them to a gallery that saw the potential in the project, and we struck a deal. I began working toward my first solo exhibition, which would open on Halloween night.

One evening, I was taking pictures on my iPhone of the prototypes. I filled an Adobe Photoshop canvas with a bold color, set it to full screen, sat the paper model in front of it, and took a picture. It was a bit of a eureka moment really. It suddenly became very theatrical. I started showing people photos of the models in this format and saw a developing trend in their reactions. I felt like it was more than just papercraft now—it gave the observer an opportunity to connect the visual with their own memories. Horror movies that we've seen as youngsters seem to really resonate with us as adults, especially

those films from the '70s and '80s. By giving a viewer a simple snapshot in a very analog format, all their memories of watching the film come flooding back. I knew at this point that the models had to be presented this way, so I spent quite some time working with a framer on developing a display case for them. The result was back-lit acrylic boxes in which the kirigami is presented. It was like creating little worlds for people to peer into. At this point, I was really quite excited about Horrorgami, but I was in no way prepared for how it would go so viral.

In the months leading up to the exhibition, I was receiving calls and emails every day from journalists. It was on *BBC News*, I had a full-page review in *Time Out* magazine, *Wired* wrote an article about it, and the exhibition was featured on io9, *ABC News*, and countless other magazines and blogs. I really felt like I was dreaming. It even got on to the front page of *Reddit—Number 13*, a delightful coincidence.

Previous Page
Venice
Detail of a kirigami set inspired by the film *Don't Look Now*.

Above
The Dakota Building
Rosemary's Baby.

Right
The Macniell Residence
Ghostbusters.

78
London
UK

Lobulo, a.k.a. Javier Rodriguez Garcia, is a papercraft illustrator originally from Barcelona, now living and working in London. He began his career as a graphic designer, working for various companies in Barcelona. But in 2009, he decided to shift his attention to illustration, leaving the design world behind him. Lobulo has since worked with a diverse range of clients, including Oprah Winfrey, Sparkle Telecom, and Tesco, and has collaborated in exhibitions around the world.

Lobulo

You worked for ten years in various graphic design studios in Barcelona. Why the transition to illustration? Does your graphic design background play a part in the way you work now?
The cause was as simple as this: Having worked for a long time for different companies, but ones with essentially the same background, I got bored with graphic design. I think designers work for too many hours in front of a screen, and breaking out of this routine is the best thing I ever did. I love working with my hands, and I spend hours thinking of how I can convert 2-D illustrations into great paper 3-D illustrations.

In any case, my graphic design background always helps me with my compositions before and after my photo shoots. Furthermore, having a foundation in graphics is key to having an understanding of typography.

What led you to start using paper in your work?
One day around Christmas, I was working on my computer, when I saw a few papers on my desk. I started to play around, cutting them into different shapes, and I ended up with a paper illustration. I took a quick photo and emailed it to my friends as a Christmas card. They loved it! Later on, I couldn't stop working with it. Paper is a cheap material that offers millions of color palettes and textures, and it's really easy to work with.

How did you develop your style, and what were your inspirations?
I think everyone develops their own style in the same way: trial and error. You need to go through that process in order to find out anything. I developed my style by getting things wrong and starting again.

My inspirations are in the day to day: the Internet, hanging out with my friends, riding my bike along the canal, a hot coffee in the morning, the books on my shelf.

Could you take us through your general working method?
Sketchbook > Adobe Illustrator > Develop the set on paper > Shooting

What tools do you use to create your work? Are there any particular paper stocks that you favor?

Right
Mr. T
A personal project
inspired by the '80s
icon Mr. T.

I probably use what you'd imagine: a scalpel and scissors, but the most important tool is the paper. I definitely don't have any paper stocks I favor, but I much prefer working with 150 gsm sheets because I find it's the perfect paper weight for 3-D illustration.

How do you go about photographing your illustrations?

I am always happy to shoot my projects myself. I use a photographer if the job requires it, but we'll always be working shoulder to shoulder because I am very meticulous with my work and need to take the photos exactly as I like them.

What has been your most enjoyable project so far?

Darth Vader is maybe one of the favorite works I have ever done. It's probably because when the editor of the magazine sent me the email with all the rules for this issue, he gave me absolute freedom to make whatever I wanted. Star Wars is probably one of my bigger inspirations. I remember the day when I went to the cinema to see *Star Wars Episode IV* with my parents, and when we left the cinema, I thought, I'm going to do something for this!

How do you manage your time, and what tricks have you discovered along the way to help you speed up the process?

Coffee is my principal tool. But my second one is practicing making 3-D models quickly. Once you have memorized it, you work so much faster.

Looking toward the future, what direction would you like to take your work?

Exhibitions, toys, and limited editions. In fewer words: continue to do just what I love to do.

Right
Darth Paper Vader
An illustration for *Gööo*
magazine.

Left
Cut into Sections
A personal project that
Lobulo created inspired
by insect anatomies.

This Page
Made by Cows
An illustration created
for Anchor showing
the natural goodness
of their butter.

Paper Shredder
A piece for *Creative Review* made entirely from paper to represent a range of different paper stocks. Photography by John Short.

84

London
UK

Chrissie Macdonald

Chrissie Macdonald is a London-based illustrator, model-maker, and set designer. Her vibrant scenes often toy with our perception of reality, exploring form and scale. She graduated from the University of Brighton in 1998, and in 2000 formed the multi-disciplinary collective Peepshow along with six friends from her course. The original group has expanded and contracted over the years and now comprises ten creatives, half of whom Chrissie shares a studio with in East London.

How and why did you begin working as a freelance illustrator?

My interview after graduating unexpectedly resulted in my first commission: a menswear fashion story for *Sleazenation* magazine. I'd seen a beautiful piece documenting empty airports in their previous issue, so I knew they were the ones to approach, although I never expected anything to come of it so quickly. The small budget went toward models and photography costs, so everyone involved worked for free, but it was definitely a worthwhile use of my time. The whole experience was such a learning curve and also a lesson in not taking anything for granted because it was a fair while later that I got my next commission.

When I first started showing my folio around, paper-cut illustration wasn't quite as prevalent as it has become in recent years, and although my work generally went down well, people didn't know quite how to use it. I was unsure how to apply my process and aesthetic to an illustration context and struggled to find an outlet for it. I ended up working in a few different areas, such as film and creating shops' window displays, in a bid to see where my work might fit. Although it was all great experience, I was drawn back to illustration and made a decision to have another crack at freelancing. Thankfully, the day I started, a commission came in to design club flyers, which gave me the impetus to keep at it.

You're part of the Peepshow Collective alongside an array of talented artists. How did this come about, and to what extent do you work as a group?

It was a bit of an eye-opener after graduating to discover how lonely it was outside of college, to lose the studio environment with such a tight-knit group of friends and shared experiences. It wasn't until a group of us assisted author and artist Graham Rawle on a large-scale installation for Expo 2000 in Germany that we discovered how fun it was working together again on such a diverse project. It helped us embrace working outside of the conventional constraints of traditional illustration, in all sorts of media, and was the catalyst in forming Peepshow.

The collective's aim was initially to encourage us to produce work outside of our usual working practice—and various day jobs—as well as promoting our work by sharing costs, setting up a website to showcase our individual work, and drawing strength in numbers.

Because the site was based on a peephole, offering a glimpse into our illustration portfolios, we chose the name Peepshow, and in September 2001, organized our first group exhibition at the New Inn Yard Gallery in Shoreditch.

We generally work on our own individual illustration commissions, coming together to collaborate on exhibitions, installations, events, and animations. We all tend to get stuck in, though with experience, we have learned to delegate different roles to

Below
Chrissie at her home in
London. Photography
by Jess Bonham.

suit our individual skills. Often a larger group will work on initial ideas and storyboards together before a smaller team or pair sees the project through to the end.

Your work explores a range of different materials, but paper seems to make quite a consistent appearance in your portfolio. What led you to start using paper in your work, and what is it about the material that attracts you to keep using it?

Paper and card are so readily available and affordable (particularly in relation to other sculpting materials) that when I began to create pieces in 3-D at college, it seemed like the logical material to use. I like that such an ephemeral medium—often used to create maquettes of something more permanent—can be captured in a photograph and become more lasting, what becomes the finished product. The restrictions of the material can also help to inform the design and outcome; I enjoy the problem-solving and the parameters involved in creating pieces from card, although I don't think the process should get in the way of an idea.

I've continued to use paper in my work, partly because over time, I've gotten better at working with it, but primarily because of the response from art directors and commissioners. Once you've established a certain style, they'll come back to you for that particular aesthetic. In a way, with each new commission, it becomes self-perpetuating.

Your work combines 3-D model-making and set design. How did you develop this style?

I began working in 3-D at university. I built a model of a petrol station to accompany a kit of parts—I'd intended for the objects to become the final artwork. In documenting the piece for the cover of the box, I included cutout photographic figures as board-game-

style pieces and used them to compose small compositions. Eventually, I realized the photographs were more interesting than the objects themselves, so I presented these as the final piece instead.

Over the years, I've developed this style of working alongside more object-based compositions. However, having photographed my own work at university, I soon discovered what an important role photography plays in communicating my ideas. More than merely documenting the object, it can enhance it. I began to collaborate with photographers to create images of my projects. I work most regularly with photographer John Short, with whom I've built a good working relationship over the years—we understand each other and generally agree on what we're trying to achieve but are also candid enough to tell each other when something isn't working.

Collaboration plays a big part in your working practice. Has this always been the case? How has working with others shaped your work?

V&A Lates
These seasonal poster and postcard images illustrate a program of themed events held in the Victoria and Albert Museum. Photography by John Short.

Right
Words
Selfridges window
display created
through It's Nice
That celebrating
the inspirational and
creative power of words
and literature.

Above
Bier
Artwork for Creative
Review inspired
by 1980s still-life
compositions that often
incorporate a selection
of unlikely objects. The
components are made
from papers of the
same name: Chocolate,
China, Ebony, Ivory,
Lager, Pils and Marble.
Photography by
John Short.

I've been collaborating for most of my career, be it with Peepshow members, photographers, or other designers and illustrators. It's hard to say to what extent working with Peepshow has influenced my work, because it's probably too much to quantify! The others in the collective have definitely helped me to appreciate and celebrate the imperfections and quirks in a piece of work or idea, because I could sometimes go too far with a neat and clean aesthetic.

Working with John [Short] has helped me to develop a visual language, creating atmospheric images that sometimes play with reality and scale. More recently, I've been collaborating with Emmi Salonen of Studio EMMI, combining her graphic design sensibilities with my 3-D

aesthetic to work on a larger scale and to create pieces that exist in the real world. I definitely see the benefit of collaboration—it helps you to step outside your usual working process and look at things differently. It keeps things interesting.

What would you say have been your most challenging projects so far?

I'd have to put the campaign I worked on for Orange up there, both as one of the most challenging and rewarding I've ever done. The entire project lasted about three and a half years, which I could never have anticipated; it was quite an undertaking. Early on, it was apparent I'd need to enlist the help of an excellent producer and skilled makers to work alongside me throughout the campaign. Thankfully, Alex Bec

Chrissie Macdonald × It's Nice That
www.chrissiemacdonald.co.uk

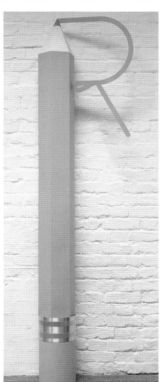

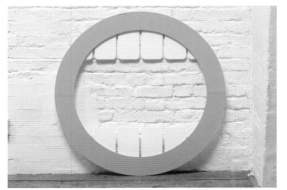

Edinburgh Fringe Festival
A series of images illustrating the different themes represented at the Edinburgh Fringe Festival. Photography by John Short.

from It's Nice That was working with Peepshow at the time, and he introduced me to some amazing designers. Together with a few others I had in mind, we established ourselves in a new, larger location and began to build.

It was my first experience managing a team, but thankfully, they were a brilliant bunch of ladies; they really helped get me through it. It was also the first time I'd ever had to let go fully enough to allow others to produce work under my name, which was really hard at first. I soon realized it was necessary, however, and was actually quite healthy for me. The client and agency would come down to the studio for regular visits to look at the work and discuss the shoots, which probably helped to cement our close working relationship. They really put their trust in John and me on the project; we were afforded the luxury and creative freedom of having our input acknowledged and respected.

Looking toward the future, what direction would you like to take your work in?
I'm enjoying working on larger-scale pieces designed to interact with the real world, which is something I'd like to do more of. I'm also creating a children's book with my sister Fiona, who's a writer. That's another avenue that I've not yet explored.

Creative Review
This cover image was created to accompany an interview with Chrissie in the same issue. Photography by John Short.

Madonna
Hand crafted paper sculptures made in collaboration with photographer Luke Kirwan that emphasize shadow and the repetition of patterns.

The Makerie is Julie Wilkinson and Joyanna Horscroft, a design duo working between London and Milan. Together, they create lavish set pieces for international clients such as Gucci, Vogue, and British Airways. Having met while studying graphic communications at Bath Spa University, the pair has developed a unique style with an incredible attention to detail and a clear passion for their craft.

Joyanna, can you tell us a little bit about your studio and your backgrounds? When did you two realize you worked well together?
A lot of very random and animated chats at university definitely gave us the first hints. We met while we were studying graphics in Bath and soon started working together on odd projects. That led to organizing a lovely third-year exhibition, which was a bit mad but was received really well, and that basically sealed the deal. But, because that would have been too easy, we then ditched each other for a year or two; Julie went off to the high-flying world of advertising, and I explored the wondrous studios of other artists. But we kept regrouping occasionally on weekends to talk about stuff that excited us. Our experiences during that time made it clear that working together and making beautiful things in our own way was the best outlet for us.

What led you to start using paper in your work, and what is it about the material that attracts you to keep using it?
I guess we're just hooked on its versatility, and love that you can create anything from it—anything! The fact that there are such beautiful textures and colors available now is really inspiring, and it's a pleasure to explore and celebrate those qualities. We're really into the sumptuous aesthetics that can be achieved by using special and patterned papers, and how prints influence the overall look of a piece.

Your work has a highly detailed and decorative style. How did this style develop, and what were your inspirations?
We like old things, treasures; things that should be preserved, such as antiques and stories. It's pretty ironic that preserving 3-D paper is almost

The Makerie

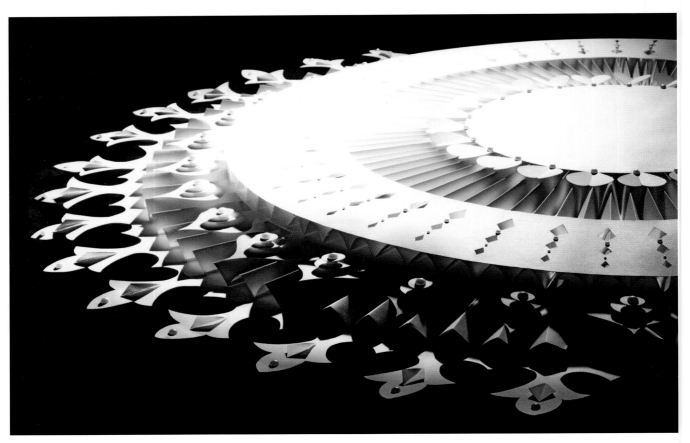

impossible—perhaps we like the challenge? Or we're just not very well? Who knows, but taking time to create something precious is really important to us, especially now—you figure out so many cool little techniques in the process, which then feed into other ideas or projects. Our overall style has always been very similar to what it is now though, perhaps just refining itself as time has gone on. The need to make pieces fast definitely helps us work out the best way to do things.

Could you briefly talk us through your general working method?

We usually start by talking about something cool we've seen recently, or an idea that we've had for a while but needs an outlet. Then we do a lot of incomprehensible drawings to help work out how each part or phase could be achieved; sometimes looking at the techniques we'll use to make them can reinforce the concept or spark a new one into life. After that, it's lots of tea and biscuits and more drawings, dividing up the work after we're clear about the outcome, and then we sit and cut for a

Madonna
Details of the intricate hand-crafted paper sculptures made by The Makerie in collaboration with photographer Luke Kirwan.

The Emerald Omar
Life-sized peacock created for Channel 4. The piece is created entirely using hand-printed Chiyogami papers, with gold foil and Swarovski crystals used for the finishing touches.

few days. Then glue for a few more. We work this way pretty naturally, talking a lot and sharing opinions on Justin Bieber when the creative chat runs low. There's also the familiar day-before panic session, but we embrace that as part of the process now—knowing things always turn out okay really helps.

What would you say have been your most enjoyable projects so far?

That's a really tricky one. Luckily there's a bunch to pick from. Apart from having Azerbaijanis hassle us, the presidential dinner in Baku was a great experience— we got to see a beautiful and unusual country and follow a huge set-design process from start to finish. The windows we did recently for Printemps in Paris were also really fun, because basically we had complete artistic freedom. There's probably an element of love and hate in every project, though learning from each one makes up for the hate part—and the sense of relief at seeing how well things go makes you feel like every one's been the best project to date.

How do you manage your time, and what tricks have you discovered along the way to help you speed up the process?

The trick to not having time run away is to be very clear about what you are going to make—that and very hard work. We often have to give up our social lives for the entire length of a project (and projects usually come in batches) and work consistently long hours, so knowing what your priorities are is important.

Also, as a team making complex or numerous pieces, it wouldn't be constructive to let personal whim take over. It's good to stay focused so everyone knows what's going on, but of course, if you think of a better way of doing something halfway through a project—which, to some degree, is every

Room 2013
A series ofsets
commissioned by
Splash Dubai based
around human body
parts. Photography by
Lucia Giacani.

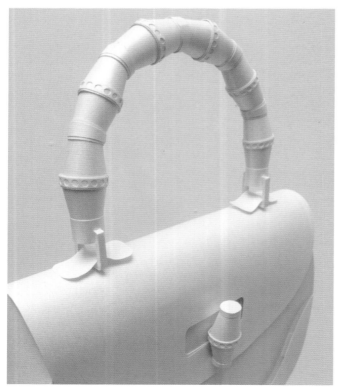

Iconic Bags
Part of a series of
six bags created for
Fabrice Fouillet's
Vogue Gioiello shoot.
The bags were exact
reproductions of the
designer classics, made
using iridescent white
papers shot on lace and
fabric backdrops.

**Crivello Flora
Catalogue**
A series of white paper
flowers and surrounding
sets created for Crivelli,
inspired by tropical
and forest flora.
Photography by Anna
Giannuzzi & Stefano
Marino.

time—then it's quicker to say something
and put it into action than to keep
plowing on.

Looking toward the future, what direction would you like to take your studio?

We really like where we're going at the
moment, so anything a little like this—
with the volume turned up—would be
great. We'd really like to involve more
new materials in our work, while still
keeping the handmade craft feel. We're
very lucky that we are often given a
lot of freedom in our paid work, which
is something we really appreciate—it
lets our personal style come through.
We'd also love to do some massive
installations in gallery spaces at some
point. That way, people could see the
work as it really exists, not from behind
a window or lens. Doing more art-based
projects would be super, and letting
that feed back into the commercial side
would be great too.

Finally, do you have any words of wisdom that you could share with people who are just starting out in this profession?

Call us. It's incredibly hard to find
talented people! If you're good at
something, and you like doing it, remind
yourself of your goals all the time,
because starting on your own is a long,
long road. Don't worry though, the good
ones definitely make it.

100

Adelaide
Australia

Stuart McLachlan

Stuart McLachlan began his career as an illustrator in Adelaide, Australia, after completing a degree in illustration and graphic design. From there, he travelled extensively and has worked in several cities around the world, including Amsterdam, Montreal, Vancouver, and Melbourne. Although active in the world of illustration, over the past few years, Stuart has shifted his attention toward paper styling, using cut paper to create images and objects for fashion, advertising, and art projects. These handmade pieces have been used extensively on the fashion runway and have been published in *Vogue*, *IDN*, and *Karen* magazine, as well as various books and journals.

Your early illustration work was quite different from your more recent papercraft creations, using pencil and paints. What led to this transition to papercraft?
This was the beginning of a new direction for me as an artist. At that point in my life, I wasn't expecting to have discovered a way of working that truly produced what I consider my own personal style. I have worked with just about every painting technique under the sun and have produced styles for which I have become well known as an illustrator. However, painting never seemed to be 100 percent me. My illustration style always contained references to past art movements, and I tended to employ several techniques instead of one that embodied me as an illustrator.

My paper art changed that—it was something that was my style, was not borrowed from anywhere, wasn't derivative of any other artist's work, and reflects 100 percent the way I think. Paper is like going back to basics: minimal drawing, often limited in color, just pure design. It's pretty primal.

My design process is very intuitive; a piece can change at any time if I can see a better result is possible. I love that the results of cutting are immediate and that because of this, one must work with decisive and deliberate thought. Funnily enough, my twin brother, who is a doctor, also works in this way as a thoracic surgeon. Like me, he uses a scalpel and as he says, "If in doubt, cut it out!" I concur with his diagnosis!

The great thing about paper is its ability to be transformed into any shape imaginable, which is great because as one of my friends says, I have the lowest boredom threshold of anyone he's ever known. The medium keeps it fresh for me.

Your work often links in with high fashion and theater, creating custom paper creations to be worn and modeled. How did this way of working come about?
There was a person who rented space in my studio, and she did PR work for several fashion labels. One of her clients, Toni & Guy, needed several costumes for the avant garde section of their catwalk show at an expo, so I produced my first major worn pieces. Very soon after that, I produced a birdcage top hat for a shoot for *Vogue* magazine, and at this point, I really saw the potential of combining the human form with paper.

I don't claim to be an expert on high fashion, but I endeavor to create an elegant classicism in what I do, so I tend to gravitate toward designers such as the timeless Alexander McQueen, Dolce and Gabanna, Prada, Chanel, and Akira Isagowa, a really amazing Australian fashion designer. My inspiration comes

Right & Below
Aurora's Night
Paper dreadnought
inspired by the
relationships between
machines and the
people of Communist
Russia. Photography by
Simon Cardwell.

from the job at hand, and I try to create works that can enhance and live comfortably in the environment that they are created for. Even though some designs are quite bizarre, they only work if they seem to exist naturally within their setting.

Because of the mixing of art and the human form, fashion and theater seem to be an obvious marriage with what I do.

Could you briefly take us through your general working method?

Generally, I visualize the concept as close to the finished image as I can. Then, I work mentally at building it and going through the construction steps that would probably take place. This is very helpful because if it is a worn piece, it has to be attached to the person and so has to be worked out in the most practical way. When you think about the practicalities, what seems initially obvious may not work, and it's better to run through all of the scenarios of what could work and what ultimately is the best path to take to achieve the best results. Approaching each facet of the build before construction this way saves a lot of time and yields smarter results. At this point, I will mock up a sketch or build a rough Adobe Photoshop version from bits and pieces of appropriate imagery until I find the right look. Depending on what I am doing, I will sometimes just start cutting and building without sketches.

Each piece is pure problem solving; it's like a puzzle that has to take strength, light, and space into account while keeping in mind a clear picture of what the end result should be.

Once the work is cut and built, then the photography has to be sorted out. With the diorama-style images that I do, I will do this photography myself. The images involving people will be photographed under my direction by someone else, and hair, makeup, and styling will have to be done by other collaborators. I choose the models and

Right
Cathedral
This piece uses the human form as an architectural anchor for the paper *Cathedral*. Photography by Simon Cardwell.

Left
Bird Cage Top Hat
Stuart's first ever wearable paper piece, created for *Vogue*. Photography by Troyt Coburn.

103

WOW Festival
A series of images from the World of Wearable Art Festival 2013. Stuart created the set for the finale of the avant garde section as well as five dresses.

sometimes do the styling myself. I intend to begin shooting these images myself but have to train in photography a little more. This said, I find that having someone else shoot the work can often take the images to another level, and I have been fortunate to work with very good photographers, models, makeup artists, and hairdressers as well as stylists.

You're currently working on a project for the World of Wearable Art show in New Zealand. Can you tell us a bit about the show? How will you be involved, and what have you created for it?

WOW (as it is called in short) is an international costume-focused art and design competition that is held in Wellington, New Zealand, which has become the city's premier annual art event.

Internationally, artists and designers are able to submit costume designs that compete in seven categories that are then built into a two-hour performance show. Instead of parading the 150 finalists' costumes out on stage, they are melded into a show that is themed to each category, which include, for example, the children's and avant garde sections. Up to 180 performers perform on a specially built stage to an audience of more than 50,000 people over the course of the three-week event.

I was asked to co-script the twenty-fifth anniversary show with the founder Dame Suzie Moncrief, who I must say is one of the most creative souls I have ever had the fortune to work with. I designed a series of hats worn by fifty children for the opening of the show in the children's category. My main commission, however, was to design the set for the finale of the avant garde section as well as five dress designs that related to it.

The finale set is huge, about 39 ft wide by 13 ft high (about 12 x 4 m) built in a duodecagon design (a polygon with

twelve panels or sides). There are two of these polygon formations, an inner and outer circle, with a 23-foot (7m) high Arabian-styled minaret tower in the middle. The set is based on the diorama kind of work that I do, and features a mad stampede of birds, animals, and insects silhouetted against another panel of wooded forest with birds flying above. The requirements of the design had to allow the set to be used for more than twenty performances and needed to be erected within a few minutes on stage in front of the audience. This required about fifty dancing guys to seamlessly position the massive structure on stage with precision, accuracy, and timing. It had to be intricate yet strong enough to hold together at that scale, which was not a simple task. More than forty performers as well as the worn finalists' costumes would then parade through the set for the twenty-minute finale.

What sort of challenges do you face working on projects such as this?

Especially with large-scale or intricate projects, you need to take into consideration how the models will stand up or how they have to be supported as you are making them. This is always the major challenge. If a section is too intricate, it can collapse in on itself. With the *Lady of the Lake* set, we had to build a ceiling trellis so that all of the sections could be suspended, then we had to place everything properly in camera frame, which was extremely tedious and time-consuming. Due to the size of the available building materials, the panels of the WOW set had to have two joins [joints] per panel. As cut-out designs ran through these joins, I had to make sure there was enough strength through these areas so that the panels wouldn't fall apart once hung.

Flight
A series based
around the concept
of flight, exploring
the combination of
silhouetted shapes with
the human form.

Billy Blue
Billy Blue College of
Design in Sydney asked
Motherbird to create a
campaign to announce
the launch of their new
Melbourne campus
depicting the principles
of thinking, making and
connecting.

Motherbird is a creative studio
based in Melbourne, Australia,
founded in 2009 by designers
and close friends Jack Mussett,
Chris Murphy, and Dan Evans. As
a studio, their output is extremely
diverse, priding themselves
on their ability to develop
conceptual outcomes through
their collaborative and often,
experimental, design process.
This has led to a range of
techniques being used in their
design work, including paper-
cutting and set design.

Jack, can you tell us about your
background and how Motherbird
came about?
We started Motherbird in 2009 after
graduating from the same university
course. We all actually met at high
school, so we knew each other inside-
out by the time we followed our dream
of opening a studio. After building a
reputation quickly in the Australian
design industry, our client base has
grown and has become quite diverse
and, in fact, global. Having been friends
for so long, we have a license to push
each other constantly to produce more
interesting work every time a new
project comes into the studio. It keeps
everybody on their toes and the creative
juices flowing.

As a studio, you've worked on a range
of different design projects, a number
of which have featured paper-based
creations. What led you to approach
these projects in this way?
The papercraft started with the Billy
Blue College of Design project. The
initial brief was very open; a variety of
concepts were available to us, and we
could use a range of different media.

Motherbird

Billy Blue
Motherbird created
three paper sets for
Billy Blue College
of Design in Sydney
to announce the
launch of their new
Melbourne campus.

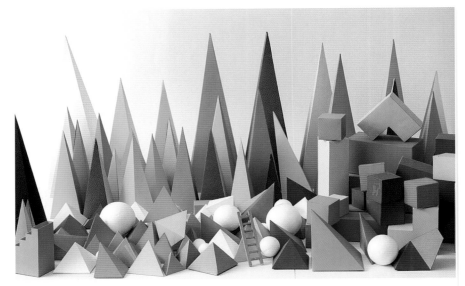

We used paper in order to convey a handmade, yet bold, colorful feel to the final piece. Carrying out a creative campaign for a design school is an extremely difficult thing to balance. You can't be too crafty, or too digital. We tried to split it down the middle. I guess the nicest thing about the campaign was when we revealed that the images were in fact handmade, rather than digitally created.

Although you don't always work with paper, a number of your projects have a feeling of tangibility, featuring bold brush marks, crumpled typography, and hand-drawn illustration. How important is this hands-on approach in your working practice?
Our hands-on approach is integral to the ethos of our studio. We try not to take the same path twice, and we experiment with new media on a regular basis. A tangible, tactile outcome is always something people can relate to—it has something very real and human about it. One of the most important things about using your hands is having the ability to get away from the computer and be an artist.

Your paper sets have a very bold and graphical style. How did this style develop, and what were your inspirations?
I'd say this developed through our love for modernist, clean, striking design. It then filtered naturally into our treatment of paper forms.

With your paper sets in mind, could you briefly take us through your general working method?
The early stages of any paper-based project will involve a lot of sketching to decide on the concept and basic form. It's usually good to establish some parameters before starting the time-consuming process of measuring, cutting, folding, and gluing paper

110

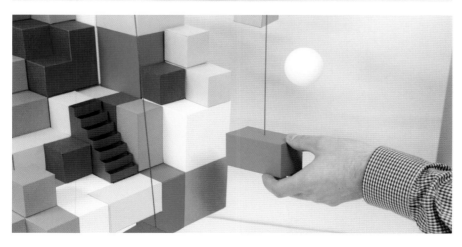

together. Depending on the scale of the project and the stakeholders involved, we may even create a 3-D vector image to make sure we get the sign-off before proceeding to the next stage.

We then kindly ask the paper supplier to inundate us with all their colored paper stock, with which we begin folding: shapes within shapes within shapes. It's all a bit like the movie *Inception*; it's very difficult not to get lost in it all. We will then usually photograph the piece in our studio because it may be built over an extended period of time, making it very difficult to move elsewhere. Once a few hundred photographs have been taken, the chosen one or two are then edited into a final graphic with any finishing color changes or additions made in postproduction.

Are there any particular paper stocks that you favor?

The colors we use are in the Spicers Optix range. We rarely stray from these because across the set, the tones have a very nice harmony to them. The work we produce for Billy Blue requires a consistency, which we can achieve through coloring.

Finally, what advice would you give to people who are just starting out in this profession?

The most important thing we have learned is not to take yourself too seriously, but seriously enough.

Motherbird 111

Shop
Front cover design for
the Hanover Edition of
SHOP magazine. This
fantasy woodland scene
was inspired by German
Porcelain. Photography
by Sam Hofman.

112
Manchester
UK

Helen Musselwhite

Helen Musselwhite's delicate, paper-cut landscapes are inspired by her love for the great British countryside. Working from her home just south of Manchester, on the border between suburbia and the countryside, she often centers her work around wild animals and rural scenes. Having completed a course in graphic design and illustration, she now creates pieces for a broad range of clients including Cadbury, Nokia, and Audi.

Your work over the years has varied from decorative furniture and jewelry design to painting, but you now work predominantly with paper. What first attracted you to the material, and why has it become such an important part of your work?
I was first attracted to paper when I was looking for something easily available and inexpensive to make a Christmas shop-window display. This was during my time as a maker of rudimentary jewelry in my friend's (far superior) jewelry store and workshop. It was when using tracing paper to make the display that I quickly realized other kinds of paper had huge potential (and that jewelry-making wasn't my forte!). Also, around this time, the "Father of Contemporary Paper-Cutting," Rob Ryan, was becoming far better known for his work. I'm sure that's no coincidence!

Paper is important to my work because it gives it life and dimension—without it and what you can do to it (fold, score, roll, curl, etc.), my work would literally be flat. I haven't (yet) learned to use a computer program to generate images, and I don't think my painting skills are up to much, so I had to find another way to work.

Your work often explores themes surrounding the British countryside using a range of layers and lots of detail. How did you develop this style, and what were your inspirations?
I'm not sure how I developed the layers thing—I suppose it's a fairly obvious step from what's ostensibly collage to layering to give depth. Perhaps one influence was a set of 3-D, framed Hawaiian scenes

belonging to a relative of mine that depicted little huts and indigenous scenes made from bark and twigs. I remember thinking how I'd like to get into the pictures. (I'd like viewers to think that about my work too, especially the house and cottages in domes—the doors are always open for that reason!)

Another strong influence, again from my childhood, was a museum near Brighton dedicated to the anthropomorphic taxidermy tableaux, made by an eccentric Victorian named Walter Potter—kittens as bride and bridegroom and other small animals as the congregation. The countryside themes are in my blood because I was born and have lived most of my life in or near the countryside. My ancestors were all country dwellers who worked the land. I use detail to make my work different. I also like to get lost in the making process, and I see detail as a craft and a skill.

You've worked with a number of photographers to shoot your illustrations. How important is collaboration in your working practice?
I love to collaborate with photographers, and I've been lucky enough to work with two great exponents of shooting paper work: Lacey and Sam Hofman. They understand how to get the most from paper artwork and are both meticulous craftspeople. Collaboration makes you think in different ways, too. Often the daily life of an illustrator is solitary, so it's great to get out of the studio and work with others who share the

National Theatre

Hansel and Gretel

written by Lucy Kirkwood.
Devised by Katie Mitchell and Lucy Kirkwood
based on the story recorded by the Brothers Grimm

Hansel & Gretel
A poster design created
for the National Theatre
depicting the story
of Hansel & Gretel.
Photography by Tom
Robinson.

ARTS COUNCIL ENGLAND
Supported using public funding by
ARTS COUNCIL ENGLAND

The National Theatre's
Cottesloe Partner

neptune
Investment Management

same goal but have alternative ways of achieving it.

What would you say have been your most enjoyable projects so far?
I do like working on advertising jobs (for the reasons already mentioned). Although they are intense and often have a short time frame, the interaction between the art directors, the photographers, and me is great and pushes my thinking and creativity. I also loved working on the cover of the *Holland Herald* magazine. I got to use some of my favorite elements: a house, trees, an owl, and deer, but I also had to include people, which is always a test. Using LEDs in the house and behind the set to light the evening sky was great, because I'd used them in self-initiated work, and I was itching to use them in a live job.

How do you manage your time, and what tricks have you discovered along the way to help you speed up the process?
I'm a bit of a night owl and find I work

Left
Happy Meals
Part of an advertising campaign for LeoBurnett LDN promoting books and the natural world in McDonalds Happy Meals. Photography by Sam Hofman.

116

better later in the day/evening (although I would dearly love to be up with the lark). I do regularly hear the Shipping Forecast!

There are no special tricks to speed up my working/making process because it's always hand-cut (and always will be). I write a lot of lists, and that helps me mentally when I can cross things off them.

Could you take us through your general working method from the initial ideas stage to the final outcome?

I write notes and key words first, then make thumbnail sketches, which I enlarge on a photocopier (because most of the time those first uninhibited and quick, free drawings are the best). Then I work them up to size as pencil line drawings. By this time, I'm also working out the layers. (It's the same with the domes and true 3-D stuff; they are really just layered paper but in the round). I've also probably got a color scheme in mind now (that's usually dictated by the subject matter or the brief). When

Above
Helen at her studio.

Left
Detail of illustration made for McDonald's Happy Meals.

Helen Musselwhite 117

Holland Herald
Front cover design for the *Holland Herald* winter edition inspired by frozen countryside, canals and traditional wooden houses.

I'm creating self-initiated work, I go straight into the final piece, but with a commercial brief, I usually have to do a mock-up of either an area of the artwork or, with the 3-D sets, a quick maquette, before I start.

Looking toward the future, what would be your dream project?
My dream project would be a children's storybook with a stop-frame animation spin-off. Designing theater sets would also be at the top of the list.

Finally, do you have any words of wisdom that you could share with people who are just starting out in this profession?
Make sure your style has something unique to you to make it stand out. Social media is very important as a means to get your work seen—use all the platforms available. No one will come looking for you unless you give them reason to, but do step away from it too—time away from the Internet is time well spent. Hard and dedicated work has its rewards, eventually.

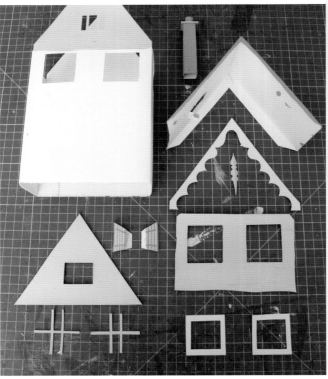

Holland Herald

SAIL AWAY

317

61

Yacht charter ❶
Sailing in Greece ❷
Forecast ❸
Climate data ❹

The long o...
early as Mar...
temperatures ...
seawater tempera...

21

Set designer and image-maker Hattie Newman creates bold and playful imagery that combines elements of both two- and three-dimensional design. Often exploring color and scale with childlike imagination, her pieces range from vast paper landscapes to intricate model villages. Hattie now lives and works in London and has a "passion for paper."

Hattie Newman

First, can you tell us a little bit about your background?

I'm originally from the Devonshire countryside. As a child, I spent many solitary hours drawing maps and making cities out of Lego, with dreams of becoming an architect. Years later, I studied illustration at the University of the West of England in Bristol and now live and work in East London as a set designer sharing a studio with a bunch of creative friends.

How important do you think your time at Bristol UWE was on your development as an illustrator?

I think it was essential to my development as an illustrator. It gave me the time and space to completely explore how I wanted to work and develop my style. I was in my own little bubble. I also think the hours I spent screen printing, book binding, and creating pop-up books improved my making skills.

Your work always has a fun and playful feel, using bright color palettes. How did you develop this style, and what were your inspirations?

My family members are very colorful, so in a way, I was brought up on color. My grandfather's surreal, sequined paintings covered the walls of my parents' house, and my mum has always had a penchant for vibrant, patterned wallpaper that definitely influenced my subconscious. As did the TV shows and films I watched growing up—especially *The Muppet Show*, *Postman Pat*, and *Willy Wonka & the Chocolate Factory*. I've always been drawn to tactile objects and characters, especially if there's something strange and silly about them.

What led you to start using paper in your work, and what is it about the material that attracts you to keep using it?

I wanted to be an illustrator, but I was never satisfied with my 2-D illustrations; I felt like I was never finished until I had brought them to life physically. Paper and cardboard were the cheapest

GQ
Part of a series of set designs for French *GQ* magazine. Photography by Lacey.

Left
High & Mighty
Hattie working on
an illustration for
Eureka magazine
depicting architectural
typography.
Photography by
Catherine Losing.

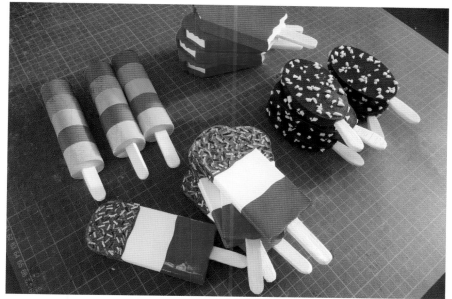

Ice Lollies
A personal project featuring a range of hand-crafted paper iced treats. Photography by Sam Hofman.

and most accessible materials, so I guess that's why I started using them. During my degree, I experimented with stop-motion animation, which led me to make 3-D puppets and sets out of paper and cardboard.

Working at quite a large scale, how do you go about planning your sets?
The client will brief me, and we'll develop a concept before I sketch out my ideas. At this stage, I often experiment and make a 3-D mock-up if there's time. I work closely with a photographer and art director, and together we decide on scale, color palette, materials, and lighting, but often the final composition won't be worked out until the day of the shoot, when the set is put in front of the camera. My favorite part of a project is seeing the set photographed. It's exciting to see it come together after having spent so much time making it.

What tools do you use to create your work? Are there any particular paper stocks that you favor?
I have a wonderful collection of scissors—each pair has its own role and personality. Scalpels, glue, rulers, and cutting mats are essential, and I'm always using my braddle and bone folder. Other useful things are my compass, Blu-Tack, masking tape, and pins. I'm a hoarder of all kinds of paper. (I have two plan chests–full, and that's still not enough space to store it all.) In terms of favorites, I have to admit I do love the Fedrigoni Woodstock range.

You've worked with a number of photographers to shoot your sets. How important is collaboration in your working practice?
It's very important that I collaborate with photographers because most of my work ends up in a 2-D context: in

Miami Motors
Still from a short animated illustration for *Stylist* magazine. Photography by Ania Wawrzkowicz.

magazines, posters, or online. I love collaborating with all sorts of creatives such as photographers, stylists, and art directors. It's fun to share ideas, create a challenge, and solve problems together. It also means that every project is different, which keeps things fresh and exciting.

What would you say have been your most challenging projects so far?
There have been a few—every project has its own challenges. I had to replicate and scale up a Herbal Essences shampoo bottle out of paper once for P&G. It had to be seven feet tall, and I only had a day to make it. It turned out to be a bit of a nightmare because the bottle has such a strange curved shape, but I got there in the end. The longest I've ever spent on a project was for *The Fedrigoni Mountains*. The paper mountains took me about a month to make, day and night! I had to score, fold, and glue hundreds of bits of card to create its geometric shape.

With projects that can be so time-consuming, how do you manage your time, and what tricks have you discovered along the way to help you speed up the process?
I estimate how long a set will take to make by comparing it with past projects. It's easy to underestimate the time I spend on my emails and the phone to clients and suppliers, so I often stay late to get things finished. If the budget allows, I will bring in one of my trusty assistants to help speed up the process.

Looking toward the future, what would be your dream project?
I have lots of dream projects. Maybe the ultimate one would be to create a friendly but strange TV show (ideally in collaboration with the ghost of Jim Henson).

124

Above & Right
Madame Magazine
A series of paper sculpture sets for *Madame* magazine. Photography by Matthew Brodie.

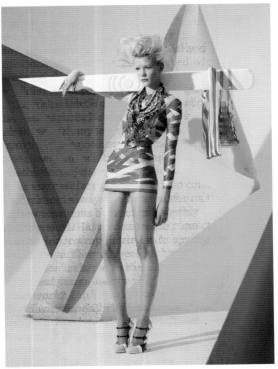

Right & Below
Made of Money
Cover artwork for the
Guardian Weekend
magazine. Photography
by Nick Ballon.

Dragon & Phoenix
Giant sculpture of a battling dragon and phoenix made for Jackie Chan. Photography by Ed Ikuta.

How did you start using paper in your work?

I've always wanted to be an oil painter, so I guess you can say that I fell into paper by accident. When I was a student at the Art Center, two of my classes simultaneously gave assignments to explore working in 3-D or in relief. We could choose any medium to work in, from clay to popsicle sticks to paper. I chose paper because I enjoyed the textural quality of paper and the challenge of making something in dimension from a flat piece of paper. For some reason, it came naturally to me, unlike painting, which I felt I was always struggling with.

You've been working with paper now for more than thirty years. How has your work developed over the years? Have you seen any changes in people's attitudes toward papercraft during this time?

I've always looked for new ways to let the paper speak for itself and not force my will upon it. I think overworking the paper takes away from the pureness and beauty of it. Of course, I use a number of other tools to work the paper, but if I were forced to, I could fit all my basic tools into my back pocket and still be able to make a paper sculpture. I guess you could say that I'm always developing ways to let more of the paper do the talking while using less of my will to make it speak.

In the past few years, people's attitudes toward paper has changed—there's now a great degree of appreciation for something that is handmade. In the early 1990s, it looked as though art and illustration were on their way out, and digital art was on its way in—big time. A lot of really great artists disappeared because they were seen as old-fashioned, working with primitive tools. Fortunately over time, people in general grew tired of instant gratification and saw the value

Jeff Nishinaka was born and still lives in Los Angeles, California— "One of the few native Angelenos around." He graduated from The Art Center College of Design in 1982 and has since become one of the world's premier paper sculptors, with a prolific career that spans more than 30 years. Nishinaka's commercial portfolio includes work for Bloomingdale's, Galeries Lafayette, Visa, and Paramount Pictures. Actor Jackie Chan, who is a close friend of the artist, owns the largest collection of Nishinaka's work.

Jeff Nishinaka

Left
Dragon
Paper sculpture of a
dragon created for the
Peninsula Shanghai
Hotel. Photography by
Ed Ikuta.

Right
Credit Suisse/Baidu
Muti layered sculpture
created for Euro RSCG.
Photography by Rob
Prideaux.

of doing it the "good, old-fashioned way."
This new-found appreciation toward
papercraft was something that came
totally unexpected for those of us who
stuck it out during those lean decades.
The really ironic part about it is that it's
mostly thanks to the Internet and blog
sites that have rekindled the excitement
in the art form.

***Your work often uses a very minimal
color palette, just playing with the
shadows and tones created through
layering white paper. How did you
develop this style, and what were your
inspirations?***
My very first sculpture had no color, it
was just white paper. My inspiration for
using minimal color, or no color at all,
comes from classical Greek and Roman
sculpture as well as from Michelangelo
and Renaissance sculpture. I think it
makes much more of a statement when
all you have to play with is light and a
gradation of shadows. I love color, but for
me, it always seemed to take away from
the sculptural quality of paper. It hid all
those beautiful and subtle shades of tone
and highlights that only an all-white
paper sculpture could display.

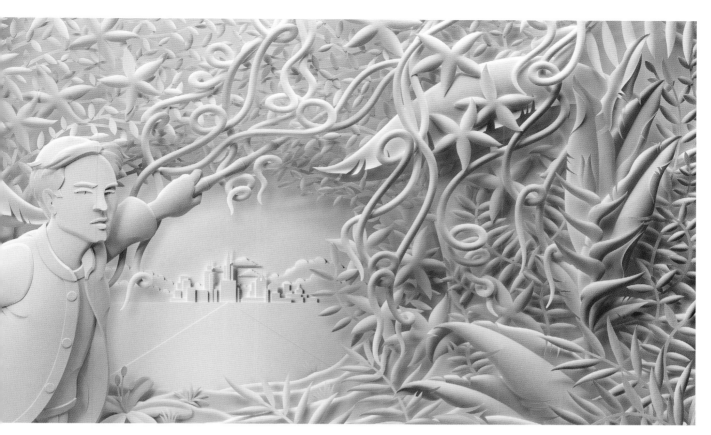

Left
Imagination
Paper sculpture
created for *Spirituality
& Health* magazine.
Photography by Ed
Ikuta.

Jeff Nishinaka 131

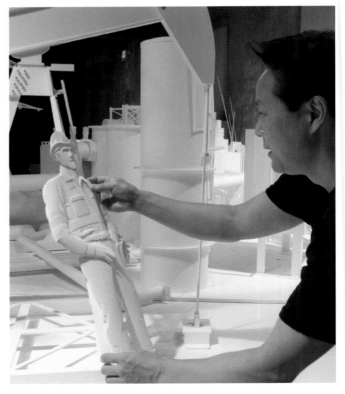

Bulwark
Jeff created this elaborate sculpture for Bulwark; an apparel company specializing in high-end, fireproof protective clothing for industries such as oil and gas, electrical, and manufacturing. The project took eight months to complete.

You have an amazing ability to treat paper like a sculptural tool that you can shape and form at your will. How do you go about creating your smooth curved forms, and what tool do you use to create your pieces?

What I use is so basic it's funny. I work with a small wood dowel like a rounded pencil, only smaller in diameter. I also use a larger 3/4" (19 mm) –diameter acrylic rod for larger curved forms. I just roll the paper between my fingers and the wood dowel for smaller curves, and my right thigh (wearing jeans of course!) and acrylic rod for larger curves. It's much easier to show rather than tell you.

What would you say have been your most challenging projects so far?

One of the most challenging projects by far would be the the large sculpture for Bulwark, which was burned to the ground for the final act.

This was a different sort of challenge. I had to mix paper sculptures of people in relief with 3-D sculptures of smokestacks, electrical structures, and oil derricks, all free-standing and able to be transported to a rock quarry so we could burn it. It was 16 ft wide by 9 ft tall by 13 ft deep (4.9 x 2.7 x 4 m). It took my team and me about 1,000 people-hours combined to build this thing that took only six minutes to burn to the ground. To my great relief, it all worked out without a single bump in the road, other than almost being rained out. The weather was the biggest problem in the end and almost saw the whole project cancelled. I don't mess with Mother Nature!

How do you manage your time, and what tricks have you discovered along the way to help you speed up the process?

Speed comes with experience. I do very little in terms of cutting corners when it comes to making a sculpture, no pun

intended! My sculptures are done when they're done and no sooner. Managing time is a matter of not wasting energy on unnecessary tasks and movement. I believe in the "economy of motion" when cutting. If something can be cut in a single long stroke, then that's the best way to proceed, especially when cutting something such as compound "S" curves. The planning and drawing of a sculpture is just as important. The time spent doing a well-planned and thought-out drawing will save more time in the cutting and sculpting of a piece. And when all else fails, there's always skipping sleep to meet a deadline.

Looking toward the future, what direction would you like to take your work in?
I would like to keep doing what I'm doing now, but I'd also like to do more stop-motion animation with my sculptures.

Finally, what words of wisdom would you give to people who are just starting out?
I'd like to say the same thing my dad told me when I was a student. He said: "Choose only one thing, and be the best at it. Don't be a jack-of-all-trades, good at everything, great at nothing."

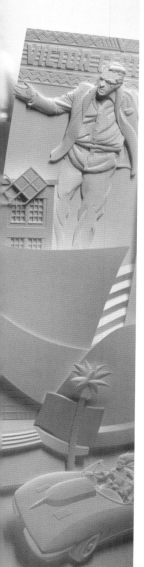

Above
Downtown L. A.
Paper sculpture
for Trammell Crow
Residential.
Photography by
Ed Ikuta.

Top
Jeff working on
one of his paper-
cut artworks.

Right
Tiger Mask
Personal project.
Photography by
Ed Ikuta.

136
Tallinn
Estonia

Eiko Ojala is an Estonian designer and illustrator living in Tallinn. Unlike the other artists in this book, Eiko's work is all created digitally, with paper and shadow only used as a visual reference. He studied Estonian nature and nature guiding and now works part-time as a nature guide, alongside his design and illustration work. Eiko has been nominated for the Illustrative Young Illustrators Award and has been featured on It's Nice That, iGnant, Trendland, and Fubiz.

Looking at your portfolio, your early work seems more design-based, and then there is a notable shift toward your current paper-illustration style. What led you to start working in this way?
I started working as a graphic designer, and illustration was just a hobby. In the past seven or eight years, illustration seemed to take over from my graphic design job. It was a natural process. But I still do graphic design work for local clients and friends.

Unlike the other artists in this book, you don't actually use paper in your illustrations. Instead you create your images inspired by paper textures and shadows. How did you develop this style, and what were your inspirations?
I lived in Australia for a few years and then took a break from any kind of creative work. Coming back to Estonia

was a fresh start for me and also for my illustration style. My first few works were portraits of my friends. They just sort of happened and seemed to work from the very first piece.

I like to study light and make every shadow myself, just like in a painting. I really enjoy that process. That's probably why I do it digitally and don't often use much real paper. I use real paper only for difficult shadows or curves.

What do you feel are the benefits of working purely digitally?
I really enjoy the process, and I'd probably not get that kind of satisfaction from cutting and gluing paper. The biggest benefit for the client is that it's easy for me to make changes.

Could you briefly take us through how you go about creating your works?
First I work with shapes. That takes

Eiko Ojala

Left
Forest
Personal illustrations for
a solo exhibition at Von
Krahl, Tallinn.

Right
In My Mind
Personal project studying
solids with liquids.

the most time. I like to keep things as
minimal as possible. I always like to
find the perfect shape for each element.
Then I'll start to think about the light
and shadows. That's when it all starts to
come to life. It's my favorite bit. Finally,
I'll work with colors. That's the hardest
and most stressful part of the process.

**If your work were a song, what would
it be and why?**
Something by Nils Frahm. A lot of my
work is born while listening to him.

**What are the current trends in
Estonian illustration? Is paper a
popular illustration tool?**
Fashion illustration is quite popular
right now, and there are a few really
good illustrators in that field, such as
Anu Samarüütel. But paper is not so
popular here. I think one paper-cut
illustrator in Estonia is enough.

**How do you manage your time, and
what tricks have you discovered
along the way to help you speed up the
process?**
I don't worry much about time. Yes, I get
faster with every illustration I do, but at
the same time, I'm always experimenting
with new things, and that takes time. To
be a great artist, you have to treat every
job as if it were your last, or first, and
forget about the time.

**Looking toward the future, what
direction would you like to take your
work?**
In the future, I'd still like to work with
light but maybe with different materials.
I would also like to experiment and mix
media, for example working with hand
drawing. I like to evolve, but I don't
want to push it. I like to think that it's
the other way around, that it is my work
that drives me forward. But I don't know
where it might take me.

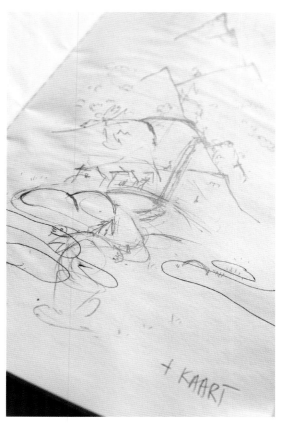

Left
Hunger For Love
Step-by-step development of an editorial illustration for Estonian weekly newspaper *Eesti Ekspress* accompanying an article about people's attachment to food.

Right
Vertical Landscape
Personal project inspired by zen paintings, studying landscapes in a vertical format.

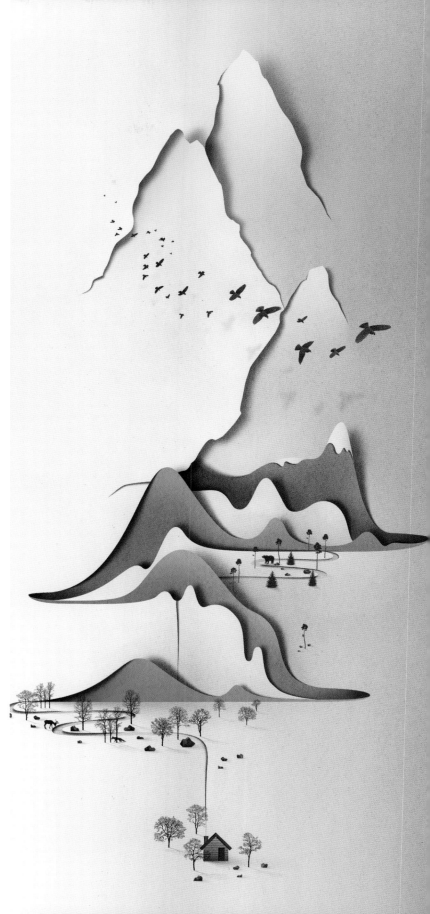

Ciara Phelan

Ciara Phelan is a freelance designer and illustrator working from Open Studio in East London. Her distinctive style combines vintage imagery with paper-cut patterns and three-dimensional shapes to create vibrant collage pieces. Since graduating from The University of Brighton in 2008, she has created pieces for a number of international clients including *Wired*, *The Guardian*, and Microsoft. Phelan is also the co-founder of Many Hands, an online store and artist collective producing contemporary prints and products.

You studied graphic design at Brighton but now work predominantly as an illustrator. Why the transition? Does your graphic design training play a part in the way you work now?

I studied graphic design because I had an A level in graphic arts. I never took a foundation course, so I didn't really know much about illustration. One of the first questions in my interview for the course at Brighton was, "Why aren't you applying for the illustration course?" which in hindsight is quite funny. I guess the main reason for my transition is that I enjoy creating imagery, and this is where my talents lie. I have never felt completely comfortable working with typographic layouts, and this has always showed through in the design work I have completed. However, all that being said, I am really thankful for my design training. I feel that I have a better understanding of compositional layout and grids, which definitely feeds into my work.

You work at Open Studio in East London. How important has working at a shared studio been in your development as an artist? Has sharing a space affected the type of work you produce?

Working in a shared studio has been a great experience and one that has definitely helped me to develop my work and confidence as an artist. Freelancing by nature can be quite an isolating and introspective career choice, so it's great to be surrounded by like-minded people who can offer advice, encouragement, and inspiration.

The main benefit of working in a large studio has been collaboration. There is a quite a wide range of people working in different parts of the creative industry, such as photography, product design, publishing, and animation. People are always looking to work on new and exciting projects in their spare time, and that can be a great way to have a break

Top
Ciara working in her studio.

Below
Reading with Kids
Part of a series of illustrations for The Guardian's *Reading with Kids* supplement.

from commercial work and develop your portfolio at the same time.

When and why did you start using paper in your work? Are there any particular projects when you remember first using this medium?

The first time I used paper was in my second year at university. I created a layered typographic image using paper stencils. I liked working with paper because it felt less restrictive than working on the computer.

Your work often combines papercraft and collage. How did you develop this style, and what were your inspirations?

My papercraft and collage mix style developed out of my love of found imagery and my passion for working by hand. When I first started illustrating, I would either create flat collages or work in 3-D with paper, and so it seemed like a natural evolution to start using the collage in 3-D and bring my work together as a cohesive whole. I source my imagery from all over. I really enjoy collecting books, so I visit a variety of places including charity shops, book fairs, bookshops, eBay, and car boot sales.

Could you take us through your general working method from the initial briefing stage to the end of the project?

The first thing I do when I take on a new project is to spend time researching the subject and finding reference imagery on the Internet, from the local library, or in charity shops. To me, this is the most important stage because research is a great source of inspiration. If I were to sit with a blank sheet of paper in front of me and try to generate ideas, the page would stay quite blank.

Once I have a clear idea and direction, I use Adobe Photoshop or Illustrator to mock up the layout and composition. I find this is a great way to see if an idea

Growth in 2012
A piece created for Colagene reflecting its aim for Positive Growth.

is going to work. Making an illustration using papercraft is very time-consuming, so I wouldn't want to freestyle because it would take twice as long. I also find this initial rough is a great way to appease a client. They often feel nervous because it is hard to visualize the final image, so this helps pacify their nerves.

The next stage is to sit down and make. This is always the most fun part but sometimes the most daunting, but I find that once I start, I usually get into a good flow. I usually construct the scene as I make it so that I have a good idea of how to scale the elements, and I can make sure that it is working. Once everything is made, I spend a few hours setting everything up and arranging it exactly as I want it.

The last stage is to photograph the scene and take it into Photoshop for some retouching. I have a small photography room in my studio, so I usually shoot there, using my Nikon D5000 and some basic lights. Once I am happy with the image, I spend several hours, sometimes

even days, retouching it. I like my work to feel quite rough, so I wouldn't retouch too many imperfections—I usually spend time getting rid of wires, blemishes, and adjusting the color balance and lighting.

What tools do you use to create your work? Are there any particular paper stocks that you favor?
The main tools I use are a scalpel, a ruler, and double-sided sticky tape; some foam board usually goes a long way too. I don't have any particular stocks that I favor, but I like using Murano because it has a slight texture to it, and there's a wide range of colors available.

How does working with a photographer compare with shooting your own work, and what effect does this have on the way you approach a project?
Working with a photographer is a real bonus because I'll be more confident that the final image quality will be great. I find that when I shoot my own work, it takes a lot more time because I have less

Ciara Phelan   145

Left & Below
Weightlessness
A paper set for the Howard Hughes Medical Institute to accompany an article in their quarterly publication *HHMI Bulletin*. Photography by Sam Hofman.

experience, and my equipment is a bit more lo-fi.

You are obviously someone who likes a challenge. Alongside your work, you also run the online shop Many Hands, and you are starting your own exhibition curation business. How do you manage your time, and what drives you as a creative?
To manage my time, I write lists—endless lists! I really like the buzz you get when you have a new project. It's always a great challenge, and I am excited to see where it's going to take me. I guess that's why I freelance—you never know what's around the corner, which is very exciting and even a bit scary at times.

Finally, do you have any words of wisdom that you could share with people who are just starting out in this profession?
Do what you love, and eventually someone will pay you for it!

Right
Friday Late
A poster advertising the V&A's Friday Late events, combining 3-D typography with collage. Photography by Emma Job.

FRI
DAY
late

WITH

MasterCard

V&A

LAST FRIDAY OF EACH MONTH
18.30 - 22.00

Celebrate contemporary art and design and take
part in free events as the V&A is transformed into
a late night venue.

ADMISSION FREE

www.vam.ac.uk/fridaylate

Can We Shall We
One of Rob's large
hand-cut artworks.

Rob Ryan is a hugely influential artist based in London. His work explores a range of techniques, including screen printing, ceramics, and painting, but he is most famous for his highly detailed large-scale paper-cuts. Inspired by Tyrolean paper-cuttings, these pieces often are based around a single hand-cut artwork featuring mirrored imagery mixed in with whimsical quotes and phrases. These paper-cuttings have led to huge artistic and commercial success, with his work being featured in countless magazines, books, and journals worldwide. He also owns a shop in East London called Ryantown, which is used as an exhibition space for his work and showcases his large range of products.

What led you to start using paper in your work?

I've always been a printmaker, so I've always worked on paper and never really board or canvas, even when I was painting. I guess I started to work with paper rather than on it. It's not a massive leap really because in screen printing, you often use cut-out stencils, so it was just a matter of making my pictures more about shape and silhouette than mark-making. Having said that, essentially my work is marks on paper because it all starts as drawing, and then I cut that line and make it solid. The process of making it what it is is more about drawing than anything.

Your work features playful decorative imagery often combined with whimsical phrases. How did you develop this style, and what were your inspirations?

Even when I was at college, I wrote. I kept lots of sketchbooks and wrote down my thoughts—they were kind of like diaries. At the same time, I did my drawings and my prints, and I suppose the two grew up in tandem, fused together, and became one. Sometimes I did pictures with no words, and sometimes I did pictures that were all words.

Regarding the decorative side of things, I've always liked and used symmetry in my pictures, even when I was painting. The works that initially drew me to paper-cutting were Swiss Tyrolean works of pastoral scenes that were folded and cut and then opened up into a symmetrical picture. But really both the decorative and the symmetrical elements of my work are devices to hold the picture together—you build the picture around them. Branches and twigs and leaves give me something to hang my picture on.

Could you briefly take us through your general working method?

I'm an avid note-taker; I write everything down—my memory is pretty awful these days, and I presume it's only going to get worse! I also sketch and doodle ideas

Rob Ryan

Rob delicately sticking down one of his intricate paper-cut creations.

I can't remember the name of the paper I use, but it comes in bigger-than-A1 sheets, it's about 70–80 gsm, and it's very smooth. Somebody told me once it was used a lot in the printing of bibles, but I don't know if that's true. I use a Swann Morton 10A blade, and I use a certain type of retractable pencil that I sharpen on fine-grade sandpaper. And I use a rubber, a lot!

Where do you get your inspiration for the phrases and poems featured in your artworks?
Just from my life.

What have been your most enjoyable projects so far?
To tell the truth, I think it always has to be the one I'm currently working on. You have to live in the present and try to do the best job you can at the time. I very much like to think that my best project hasn't happened yet. I really genuinely don't think that there's something I've done in the past that is better than something I'm yet to do. That's what keeps you going.

Your paper-cuts seem extremely time-consuming. What techniques do you employ to help you speed up the process?
My workload is really intense, so I don't really do paper-cutting anymore. It doesn't really matter whether I cut them out or not because it just involves following a line, and my eyes aren't too good anymore either, so it's become quite difficult. But speaking from previous experience, I can say that there's no point holding on to a blunt blade—change them at least every 15 minutes. Move the paper to your advantage so it's easier to approach. Cut the smallest bits out first and the largest bit last so it is structurally stronger while you're working on it.

as they come to me. So I suppose that's the initial stage. Then I'll very loosely gather all these things together and start to have the beginnings of an idea for a picture. And then I draw. I do sketches, and I throw them away and do more, and then I'll draw it up as a paper-cut and see how it looks. It'll get it cut out and then sprayed (all my pieces start as white pieces of paper and are colored using spray paint). Then I'll go back and do it again and improve it. You rarely nail it on the first hit, but that's how it goes.

What tools do you use to create your paper-cuts? Are there any particular

I Can't Forget
Personal project.

MOONS CIRCLE PLANETS
AND PLANETS CIRCLE STARS
STARS AND GALAXIES ROTATE ETERNALLY
AND YOU AND I CIRCLE EACH OTHER
FOR YOU WILL ALWAYS BE MY ENTIRE UNIVERSE
AND IF YOU WANT ME — I WILL ALWAYS BE YOURS

You Are My Universe
Personal project.

I Opened My Heart
Personal project.

Alongside the paper-cut work, you also create and sell a large range of products including mugs, tiles, pillows, and accessories to name but a few. How do you manage your time?

I manage my time by trying to do as much as I can in a day! Like anybody else, I get distracted—I play music, and I go on the Internet. Time management isn't something I'm particularly great at, but I mustn't be that bad at it because I do lots of projects. The main focus for me is a deadline. If a project has to be done by a certain time, then I'll try to do it. The hard part is trying to juggle all of my self-initiated projects, such as designing new products for my shop, around more commercial commissions. The reason I make products is that I want people who like my work to be able to have a decent slice of it, even if they haven't got a big budget. Rather than spending a lot of money on a print, you can get something cheaper—but it still comes handmade straight from my studio.

I also have a really great team, and they help to manage my time. I have people who post out online sales, people who deal with emails and computer-based stuff, and screen-printers. They all enable me to just sit at my desk and draw. That's how I manage my time best.

Looking toward the future, what direction would you like to take your work?

In the short term, I'm working on a trilogy, a set of three children's books. I've just delivered the first one, and they're quite wordy, which is quite a

Once cut out, Rob will spray paint the paper cuts in a single color.

challenge for me! I don't know if it'll work, but you have to try.

In the longer term, I would like to take my work in a direction that might surprise me. For the past ten years, my work has been mainly about shape, it's been quite monochrome, and it's been about silhouette. Sometimes, I think that I might want to burst out of those constraints, not that I find them particularly constraining. But I do sometimes feel that I might return to painting, who knows? I might even do sculpture! One day, I decided to pick up a scalpel and cut paper instead of drawing on it, so equally I might decide to pick up a paint ;brush and say, "I don't want to do this paper-cut thing anymore." Just in the same way I picked up a scalpel, I might put one down and pick something else up. But it doesn't make any difference what medium I work in, so long as I hold on to my spirit, and my work still has an emotional impact and a vivacity to it. That's what has run through my work since I started at art college. Your work is part of who you are, and how it manifests itself is just a load of stuff.

Finally, what advice would you give to people who are just starting out in this profession?

I don't really have advice for anybody because I think if you're hanging on advice from someone, then you shouldn't be doing that thing in the first place. I know that might sound a bit harsh, but there should just be a drive within you to want to get on anyway.

I can give one bit of advice—keep all of your receipts, and make sure your books are in good order. Sort your tax out, and pay your National Insurance contributions from the get-go so when you start doing a bit better, you don't have to go back and catch up.

But I don't really know what anyone else should do; half the time I hardly even know what I should do!

Vices
A set of paper portraits
of the Shotopop team.

Shotopop is a creative studio based in East London, founded by Casper Franken and Carin Standford. Their work explores a diverse range of design and illustration styles, including motion and interactive design, typography, and infographics, as well as digital and tactile illustration. As a studio, they have produced commercial pieces for clients such as Converse, Google, and Nike, and in 2012, they won a Silver Award at the 2012 European Design Awards in Helsinki for an Alzheimer's awareness campaign they created with Ogilvy & Mather in Düsseldorf.

What are your backgrounds, and how did Shotopop form?

It started as a spark from Casper, was funded by the super-kind Roelof, and was supported by an almost-wife, Carin. That spark mutated into an interest, the interest was recombobulated into a word, and the word stuck. Shotopop was born, but at that point was still just a word. A few years and a few fuck-ups later, a studio got attached to the word alongside some initial pictures, dreams, and a vague idea of how to progress. Add in a laid-back skater named Mike, a cat, and a ninja illustrator (the great Shan Jiang), and we are where Shotopop is today.

As a studio, your work encompasses a range of different styles, from infographics and motion design to digital illustration and papercraft sets. What is the cause for the diverse range of styles? Is it a conscious choice to have your hands in many different fields?

Casper and Carin, who started the company, studied a course called Information Design, which touched on everything from illustration and design to photography and animation. In starting the company, our background enforced our approach to touch on all these various fields. As we grew in size, we also garnered talent who had similar interests. While some people have a greater focus on, say, traditional illustration and its use in animation, others have more technical animation know-how or a design focus, while yet others have a combined love for paper and illustration. As you might be able to tell, illustration is always at the core of what we do, and experimentation encircles that core.

Your work explores a range of different materials, but paper seems to make quite a consistent appearance in your portfolio. What led you to start using paper in your work, and what is it about the material that attracts you to keep using it?

Shotopop has always been about exploring and experimenting. Paper was one of those experimentations that stuck, for a few reasons. It's lying around our studio most days, so it's easy to get our hands on, and it's cheap and malleable. If people are looking to create illustrations with realistic shadows, it's easiest to create them in the real world rather than imitating them in Adobe Photoshop, which, more often than not, just looks fake. And it's kinda therapeutic, sitting and cutting for hours. We also get to exercise our photography skills and experiment with lighting, and paper just generally has a nice crafted appeal, which we love.

Your papercraft work is very graphic, using bold shapes and colors. How did this style develop, and what were your inspirations?

The style has developed over a few years. Essentially, we have two paper-cut styles, but one which we feel is much more

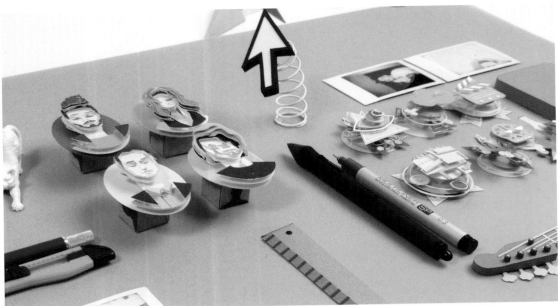

Left
Vices
Photographing a set of paper portraits of the Shotopop team.

Right
Push the Sky Away
Self-initiated project. Photography by Sam Hofman.

Below
Voodoo
Self-initiated project starting off with flat vector designs which were used as templates for the paper creation.

Shotopop! I guess what really cemented our current—and favorite—style was a project we did for ANTA and the Chinese Basketball Association that really forced us to look at the paper medium in a unique way and figure out how to use 3-dimensional space using flat planes. That was the project we feel changed how we used paper and which we feel differentiates our work from other paper artists. This style is much more graphic because it is based in design as opposed to our other style, which is more based in the re-creation of real-world objects. We still have a few projects in this "real-world" style—it's great for projects where the client wants various perspectives of a single object, for example, because the paper builds can be viewed from any angle. However, our other style, and the one that we are trying to develop more, allows us to really push boundaries of paper art and differentiate ourselves in quite a saturated market.

With your paper set work in mind, could you briefly talk us through your general working method?

We always start with a brainstorming session and list things that fit the brief. This process often involves pulling a variety of references from a range of sources to help spark ideas. Next, we sketch. This usually goes on for a few rounds of revisions and will often involve a color sketch as well. We always aim to get full sign-off on the sketch phase because

NEVER HIDE

once we go into the cutting phase, it gets much more difficult to make amendments. The color sketch really helps with this because paper colors can often be quite limiting. Once we receive sign-off, we move into the vectorizing stage. We make vector paths for all the elements, split these into colors, and print on our selected paper. Then the cutting starts. We like to cut everything before building, so that essentially, we have all the pieces of the puzzle ready to go. Once the cut is done, we piece everything together, photograph it, and then carefully retouch it.

What tools do you use to create your work? Are there any particular paper stocks that you favor?

Our tools range from software such as Adobe Illustrator and Photoshop to craft knives, glue and scissors, to cameras and lights.

We have our favorite tools for each stage, but for the actual build, we couldn't live without our forceps and glue brush. A lot of our work is really fine, and for handling pieces that are often less than

one millimeter wide, forceps and a tiny brush for applying glue are essential. In terms of paper stock, we like to experiment, so we don't really have favorites. We just don't like papers that change color when you apply glue to them.

What would you say have been your most challenging paper projects so far?

I guess the ANTA/CBA project was the most challenging because we essentially had to come up with a new style and way of working with paper within a very short time frame. Also, the project required us to supply a file that could be re-created in China, which was certainly something we had not done before.

How do you manage your time, and what tricks have you discovered along the way to help you speed up the process?

As they say, practice makes perfect. There really isn't too much you can do to speed up the process other

than getting quicker at cutting and pasting. Paper-cut illustration is just very time-consuming, so we always try to manage client expectations regarding the time frame. Over the years, we have tried to streamline the process, but it still takes time. We have even tried the laser-cut route, but that leaves burn marks on the paper, which isn't very desirable—it makes the retouching phase much longer.

Finally, what advice would you give to people who are just starting out in this profession?

1. Grow a pair.
2. If you think having a baby means you won't sleep, try starting your own company.
3. Get an accountant! Please, don't lie and say you did math at school.

Once you've accepted the hard truths, you'll realize that working for yourself will be more rewarding than ever working for anyone else. You get to do things your way, without a middleman, and that is just awesome!

Left
Anta
Shotopop were commissioned by JWT Shanghai to create a set of in-store displays using Anta shoe boxes.

Right & Below
Hack a Chuck
Shotopop was asked to "hack" a pair of Converse trainers as part of a campaign through Creative Social.

162
Amsterdam
Netherlands

Mandy Smith is a sculptural artist based in Amsterdam who enjoys re-creating varied elements and worlds through challenging the inherent simplicity of paper. Taking inspiration from both the fantastical and the everyday, she creates magical sculptures for animation, fashion, and theater that she hopes will stir emotions and bring people into a world outside of their own. Since graduating from Central Saint Martins, Mandy has directed a highly praised short film, made models for the art department on Tim Burton's *Frankenweenie,* and has worked with a variety of clients, including Coca-Cola, Waterstones, and Velvet. She was also selected as "One to Watch" in *Creative Review* and *Frame* magazine.

Can you tell us a little bit about yourself and your background?
I am originally from the Wirral, Merseyside. Since I was little, I have always loved both math and art, so I have always wanted to do something that uses elements of both. I used to play with paper (especially before starting school), but I never really considered it as something I could do when I got older. So I went to London to study graphic design at Central Saint Martins, where I specialized in advertising. I worked in advertising for a few years (at W+K and 180), then did a drafting course for film and TV art direction at Pinewood Studios before I moved to Amsterdam. I got some experience in film working for a month on Tim Burton's *Frankenweenie.* After that, I decided I wanted to change direction, so I left advertising and went into the production end of things. I love it for its constant puzzle-solving, while at the same time, being really craft-based and creative. It's just good to use your hands on a daily basis and then look down and think, "Sweet, I made that!"

What led you to start using paper in your work, and what is it about the material that attracts you to keep using it?
When I was working in advertising, the recession hit lots of its agencies,

Mandy Smith

Left
Flowerbox
Mandy setting up her
still life paper set.
Photography by Leon
Hendrickx.

and there was a time when not many
briefs were coming in. I was doing some
research for inspiration and noticed
papercraft popping up on blogs. It
made me miss what I used to do when
I was little—making things outside of a
computer. I was living in such a beautiful
city, and I thought I should make
something that represented my views
about where I lived, so I created a paper
house. I used this piece to experiment
and work out how good paper was at
holding complicated forms, creating
textures, and how structurally sound it is.
It turns out it takes many forms readily,
and you can use multitudes of layers to
create textures. You can control paper
because it cuts easily, and you're able to
add small details without any trouble.
It holds its shape if you are patient with
your glue too. The best thing about paper
is that it comes in many colors and is so
accessible, which means I can work in a
variety of places. All I need is a scalpel,
glue, and a cutting mat, and I can be
creating anywhere. It also makes such
lovely shadows in the right light; you can
get such a sense of depth without needing
much material at all.

**_Your work explores the mixture of
fantastical themes with everyday
objects. How did you develop this style,
and what were your inspirations?_**
I love math, so when I'm doing my own
pieces that aren't commercial, I love to
test and create new shapes. It's fun to
make things that are regular, but it's
more fun and more of a challenge to make
things that are skewed—the more skewed
things get, the more out of this world
things seem. It's nice to build things that
people aren't used to seeing. I love it
when I see something that looks unreal,
so I to try to create something a bit
different for other people. I use everyday
objects to ground a scene, which gives
me room to experiment in other ways
while still giving people the context of
a location. My inspirations: MC Escher,

Right
The City
A paper city playing with colored acetate to bounce different light out of and around the buildings. Photography by Leon Hendrickx.

Right
The City
A paper city playing with colored acetate to bounce different light out of and around the buildings. Photography by Leon Hendrickx.

Below
Tonka Tom Magazine
Mandy was invited to create a sculpture for an exhibition inspired by *Tonka Tom* magazine. The dress is made from 650 cocktail umbrellas covered with sections of the magazine. Photography by Leon Hendrickx.

Gaudí, Tim Walker, and of course, Tim Burton.

If your work were a song, what would it be and why?
Hmm, I love "The Carnival of the Animals: The Aquarium" by Camille Saint-Saëns. It's just so dreamy and makes me think of being somewhere bigger. I'd love for my work to one day match the place that this song takes me to.

After graduating, you worked as a model-maker on Tim Burton's film Frankenweenie. What was it like working with Mr. Burton, and how has this experience shaped your own work?
Yes, I was very lucky. I had built my paper house and had directed my short paper movie, which also featured a twisted house. I was dying to get some experience in film to see what it was like, and a friend sent *Frankenweenie*'s art director my first few pieces. They had already crewed up, but I was able to come on the set for a month and work with the draftsman to build a scale version of the interior of the windmill (to check its design before it went to the workshop to be built at full size!). It was such a great experience to see how the cogs of film work and meet such passionate people. I didn't see Tim but got to chat to and be introduced to the people who work in animation. The best part of being involved in the film is that now, when I'm at Clapham Road Studios working on pieces, I meet the same people I met

Mandy Smith 165

Below
Actimel
Print campaign for
Actimel through RKCR/
Y&R. Photography by
Sam Hofman.

on that movie. Because I love to design and model-make, I realized that I'd love doing shorts and commercial work. The thing was that the bigger the job, the fewer bases you cover personally, so I decided, for the time being at least, not to pursue a career in film.

Could you briefly take us through your general working method?
I'll either sketch something in Adobe Photoshop, do some sketches by hand, or both, and then just follow what I have drawn. For personal pieces, I have time to make changes, for example, if certain elements are creating too much shadow, or not enough, I can make alterations. It's nice to build up a scene and add details as I go. It's fun to experiment with new textures too, so I'll try to find or create a pattern that I'll use to cover an environment or character, which will help make a scene more rich. I like making things that people can look at more than once and still enjoy, so the richer the environment, the more people will return to look.

You have created some quite stunning animations for the likes of Toyota and TED global, and earlier in your career, you also worked on a number of music videos. How did you get into moving image work, and how does this kind of work compare with your still print projects?
I love animation and bringing still things to life. I suppose it comes from my background in advertising. Print shoots are lots of fun, but with TV and animation, the teams are bigger, so I get to meet and work with more people. The hours are longer, but you get a bigger rush when you look back and see everything you have created. Right now though, I'm working on a few print pieces because I haven't done so for a while. Two are conceptual, but I want to make one project themed around a fairy tale. My portfolio has definitely shifted

Above
Gramophone
Personal project.
Photography by Leon
Hendrickx.

toward TV, but I still love print, so I'm really looking forward to doing these new personal pieces!

What would you say have been your most challenging projects so far?

I've just come back from New York, where I art-directed a spot for Special K. As well as doing the normal design work, I had to work out ways to best animate paper in order to make a variety of nice transitions from geometric and boxy forms to elegant shapes. It involved the most research I think I've ever had to do into paper to find forms that not only looked nice but could also be animated. My brain actually hurt from thinking!

How do you manage your time, and what tricks have you discovered along the way to help you speed up the process?

Make things in bulk! Projects always take longer than you think, and you'll always need more things than you think. For example, the first time I made flowers to cover a patch of grass, I needed three times more than I had anticipated I would. Also, I have come up with nice simple techniques to create textures; I use a similar pattern with, say, the tree trunks I make, which lends a familiar style to many of my pieces.

Looking toward the future, what direction would you like to take your work?

I'd love to do more art shows—I'm working toward one at the moment—but also some more editorial work would be nice. I want to keep making fantasy worlds for people and hopefully build a portfolio that just grows in size, scale, and skill. One ambition of mine would be to one day work with Tim Walker. Also, if I could get back into film and design a set or even a one-off bespoke piece, that would be amazing!

Paint & Splash
Personal project.
Photography by Olivia
Jeczmyk.

Fideli Sundqvist

Fideli Sundqvist is a Swedish prop designer and paper-cut artist based in Stockholm. She graduated in 2011 with a degree in Graphic Design and Illustration, and in that same year debuted with her book *Birre, where are you?* which won first prize in publishing house Opal's contest for picture books. She has since gone on to build up an impressive portfolio filled with her wonderful paper creations inspired by everyday existence.

Firstly, can you tell us a little bit about yourself and your background?
I was born and raised in Uppsala, a small university town about 40 minutes north of Stockholm. My mother is a potter and artist and my father is a scholar who often worked from home. So you could say that I grew up with two parents whose work and interests overlapped, and who worked on their own time. The fact that I can choose how to spend my working day allows my work and passion to merge. That's what I've experienced since I was young and so have never thought about my profession as conventional "work."

When I was about fifteen years old, I became very interested in music. I made my own music and played in bands and collected vinyl records. It was by collecting these records that I began to see illustration and design as an art form —I had never seen it in that way before. One album's artwork really made a huge impression. It was a real eye-opener and I was completely mesmerized. Its cover gave the impression of being an old book, with illustrations carved in linoleum.

This is where my interest in cutting began. My mum and I took the train to Stockholm and bought all the material I needed for linoleum cuts. I became

Ibis
A range of paper sets as
part of a campaign for
Ibis Styles. Photography
by Olivia Jeczmyk.

swallowed up in the craft. I then began
to cut a series of images that were about
a boy who lived in a lighthouse with all
his longings and dreams.

How did these experiments with linocuts eventually lead to your working with paper?

Both in terms of craft and graphic
expression, the linoleum technique is
quite similar in many ways to my paper
cutting. Then, when I was in my first
year at art school, my brother went to
China as an exchange student and came
home with a book of paper-cuts (real
silhouettes in plastic pockets). I was
eighteen years old and completely moved
by the technique. The thought that
someone could work in so much detail
and dedicate so much time to it really
touched me. So I started to make my first
silhouettes, which was one of the most
fun things I had ever done. From then on
I thought much more about paper-cuts
than linoleum.

Shortly thereafter, I discovered a
book of Rob Ryan illustrations in a
shop in London. I was really astounded
by his poetic images. I think that
handcrafts really inspire me. You can
manipulate paper in a variety of ways,
its function and its style. I liked making
the linoleum cuts very much, but I
thought that the results were too rustic
and old-fashioned. With paper, I could
get an airier, modern feeling, which is
important to me. As I worked on more
3-D projects, I felt even more strongly
that paper cutting went hand in hand
with what I want and strive for.

What led to your transition from creating two-dimensional to three-dimensional paper-cut artworks?

My two-dimensional paper cuts were
really just another type of drawing, and
I had no idea that I would be able to
build three-dimensional illustrations
with paper—I had never seen that kind
of image before. I remember the first

3-D project I did: a product with folding animals. I was very excited about the transformation from a flat sheet to a three-dimensional object. I was very fond of it, but I did not know how to use it. What was it? A sculpture, a product, or an illustration?

At the same time, I started thinking about what to do for my final project at school. I spent weeks and months thinking about what I wanted to do, but I never felt that I really loved any of the ideas that I came up with. But then one evening I imagined a 3-D set in my mind that made for an interesting illustration context. I was very curious and expectant to develop what I had in my mind. It felt so right, even before I had started doing it.

Your work explores the themes of everyday life using bright but sophisticated color palettes. How did you develop this style and what were your inspirations?
I tend to find inspiration in a lot of Japanese design, and in some fashion

designers. When I find it hard to find the right colors for a piece, I usually start Googling. I can often, almost straight away, think, "This is good, this feels right," but sometimes it's hard in the sketching process on the computer to find exact color matches. When I go to buy paper, I usually put together color palettes in the shop, because it is easier to get the feeling of it when you see it there and then.

When it comes to creating shapes and style, I don't think I'm able to be so precise—it just seems to turn out the way it turns out. There always seems to be a common thread to the lines and shapes I make, which is both good and bad. For a while I hated it, but now I feel more comfortable with it. But I have found out that, by experimenting with color, I can control the feel of a piece, while the shapes and lines are still made by my own hands.

Could you take us through your general working method?
I mostly work with briefs and the client

Winter City
Storefront decoration
for Malmstenbutiken's
Winter season.
Photography by
Helena Karlsson.

usually has a pretty clear idea of what they want. So first I'll go to meetings and we'll discuss the idea, color, size and composition. Then I start sketching and writing in my notebook. Once I have quite a clear idea of what I want to do, I make pretty accurate sketches in Adobe Illustrator—these will be very similar to the final piece. These sketches bounce back and forth with the client, which I think works really well. I used to do sketches on paper but it took such a long time to amend them, or change the color scheme. As soon as the sketches are approved, I start to build. Now that I've been working for some time, I can convert them to 3-D in my head without having to make physical sketches.

The sketching part is the longest part of the process. When I do my own projects I spend the most time thinking about ideas. Once I've decided what I'm going to do and know how I want it to look, the cutting stage often goes smoothly and is the fun bit, even though it usually takes a while to start cutting. But as soon as I've started, I feel like I become a little paper-cutting machine.

When all items are complete, they are packed and it's time for the photography. Most of the time my works are photographed in studios by professional photographers, alongside the client and me. Once the photos are taken my work on the project is done.

What are the benefits of working with photographers to shoot your works?
I thought initially it would be great to shoot my works myself, but as it is it feels good to focus as much as I do on the piece. I work with different photographers. It has always gone very smoothly—I respect their profession greatly. I think there's a big difference in the final image if it's been taken by a studio photographer, rather than by someone like me. It all depends on what kind of image you want, in what context, and what you want to communicate.

I also enjoy working in a small team; my work is quite lonely so it's nice to spend these long studio days together.

Earlier you mentioned about your interest in music from an early age. If your work was a song what would it be and why?
Hmm, that's a nice but hard question. Music is a huge inspiration and often a starting point for my work. The first linoleum cuts I did were almost translations or illustrations of the music that was important to me in my teens, artists like Bright Eyes and Patrick Wolf. I guess that Bright Eyes has had the most important impact on me — or maybe Neil Young. A song that reflects my work today is one that I've only just discovered: "I Am Your Singer" by Wings from the album *Wild Life*.

What would you say have been your most challenging projects so far?
My most challenging project was probably my final degree project because everything was so new for me—working on it felt so lonely. I had so much self-doubt and was so unsure of how the piece would turn out because I had no reference points at this stage: how I would make it, what it would look like. I just had an image in my head. It was also an important and nervous time in my life. Soon I'd have to finish university and start living a life in the real world.

Working by hand can be quite time-consuming. How do you manage your time and what tricks have you discovered along the way to help you speed up the process?
It does not take as long as people think, or rather, I think I have an ability to work super-effectively and accurately when I have some time pressure. I have learned a neat way to create a schedule for a project. I write a to-do list with everything that must be done: the paper that needs to be bought, a list

Left
Three-course
Part of a three-course menu built out of paper for *Plaza* magazine. Photography by Olivia Jeczmyk. Styling by Saša Antic.

Above
Tilly & Gul
Illustrations for a children's book created as part of Fideli's bachelor project.

of meetings that need to be arranged, and a list of the pictures with the exact items that will need to be made. Maybe it sounds a bit boring, but it is so easy for me to make a big mess of it all in my head (and on my desk!), so this is really helpful. And I really like crossing out jobs that I've done on the list. It works as a motivation to carry on working. The more you plan and know exactly what you're doing, the better the chance of getting things done and staying in a good mood.

Looking toward the future, what direction would you like to take your work?

I would like to work more on artistic projects. I hope I'll become better known and move outside of Sweden. And I think I will move further away from the "sweet" expression of paper, still working with my hands, but exploring other materials. I can even imagine working in teams and collaborating with different disciplines, including music, theatre and stop-motion. Simply put, making fun and exciting projects!

Finally, what words of wisdom would you give to people who are just starting out?

I think a lot of it is about spending time on what you do. Start making, keep your work and make things clear—all of that is hard but it's so important. A lot of people have great talent and a lot of ideas but do not push themselves, or make things clear. So just start, and very quickly you'll have been working with what you love for hours, weeks, and even years! It makes you happy.

Back to Basics
A personal project
mixing retro technology
with a modern and
vibrant color palette.

176

Nancy

France

Zim & Zou

Zim & Zou is a French studio based in Nancy formed by Lucie Thomas and Thibault Zimmermann. When just twenty-five, the duo met while studying graphic design at art school and later decided to join forces. The studio likes to approach design in a contemporary manner, experimenting in various fields such as paper sculpture, installation, graphic design, and illustration. They have also become well known for their bold imagery and vibrant color palettes.

Thibault, can you tell us a bit about your backgrounds and how Zim & Zou formed?
We met while studying graphic design at art school. After the diploma, we worked as freelancers with our own clients, but we helped each other so much on every job that we decided to team up.

You both studied graphic design but now work predominantly as image-makers. Why the transition? Does your training in graphic design play a part in the way you work now?
Yes, you're right—today we don't really feel like we're graphic designers. I guess our initial training led us to find our style as illustrators. Now, I think our graphic design training plays a part mainly in the way in which we compose the installations.

What led you to start using paper in your work, and what is it about the material that attracts you to keep using it?
We felt like we needed to get away from our screens and start working with real materials. That's where paper came in; it's a material with an infinity of shades, sizes, thicknesses, and textures. It's quite a cheap material that almost everyone can access in one way or another. We find that paper gives an illustration warmth and depth.

Your work is extremely vibrant, using bold colors and forms. How did you develop this style, and what were your inspirations?
We started using our particular color palette while working on the *Paper Game* project for which we re-created two Game Boys out of paper. The first one was a scale replica, with the Game Boy gray color scheme. We found it was quite a good reproduction, but with a flashy new harmony of colors, the project took a whole new direction. We found it very interesting to create as true a reflection of the original as possible, but with a totally different color scheme. We then tried to explore different colors and treatments. Our work is always inspired by a lot of things; we always try to be aware of our personal environment as well as the world in general, so everything we see can be a source of inspiration. We're very curious people in everyday life.

Could you briefly talk us through your general working method, from the initial ideas stages to final outcome?
After receiving a commission, we start talking about concepts, then we draw

our ideas, considering the materials we'll be using and all the technical aspects involved in working with them. Once the concept has been chosen by the client, we begin creating the pieces. That probably takes the longest because we like to work by hand; we don't usually work on a computer. When the elements are finished, we install them for the photo shoot in our studio, or at a professional photographer's studio if the project has a bigger budget.

Depending on the kind of installation we're working on, it can take a lot of time to build the set, especially if we have to hang elements.

You are based in Nancy in the northeast of France. What is the current illustration scene like where you are? Is paper a popular illustration tool?

Here in Nancy, there is a very dynamic graphic design scene; it's home to one of the last galleries to exhibit graphic design: MyMonkey gallery. Paper is not really well represented in illustration because Nancy is a quite small city, so the art form remains rare in the area. Thanks to the Internet, we can work on an international stage, but we often have to travel to Paris for photo shoots and meetings.

What would you say have been your most challenging paper projects so far?

Our *Back to Basics* project was really challenging. The main reason was because of the scale of the objects. We had to find out the actual measurements of a selection of vintage electronics. We had a few on hand, like a Polaroid camera and a videotape, but the big phone and an old-school camera were really hard to find! The "investigation" process took a while before we could start modeling the objects.

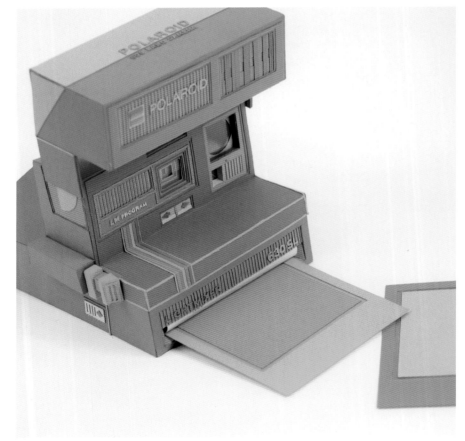

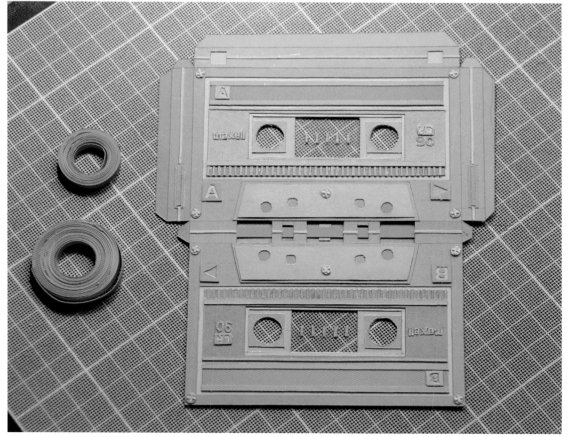

Back to Basics
Detail shots and
making-of imagery for
this personal project.

Chef's Masks
A series of masks for the
thirtieth birthday of the
gastronomic restaurant
Au Bon Gîte. Each mask
represents the various
ingredients used to cook
a different recipe.

Cabinet de Curiosités
A personal project
exhibited at Pick Me Up
Contemporary Graphic
Art Fair in London.

How do you manage your time, and what tricks have you discovered along the way to help you speed up the process?

We're always trying to be more precise in the planning stages before we begin the modeling process. We produce accurate roughs to avoid late changes. When we're cutting shapes, we try to align them on the paper sheets and then cut them in batches.

Looking toward the future, what direction would you like to take your studio?

In the future, we would really love to keep working on window displays; we love the fact that people can see our craft directly—there's more complicity between the viewer and the project that way. We would love to keep exhibiting in France but all over the world too. Being able to travel thanks to what you love to do is really a great opportunity.

Finally, what words of wisdom would you give to people who are just starting out?

We'd just say something very commonly heard but still so true: Believe and take pleasure in your work. In our opinion, there is no right or wrong answer in art. You just have to understand why one answer might be better than another. Put briefly, we all started from nothing—so just go ahead!

Left Page
The Future of Food
Cover illustration for
Icon magazine inspired
by 3-D food printer
technology.

Right Page
New Tysons
Personal project.

About the Author

Left
To Climb a Mountain
Part of a series of illustrations created for Nordea Private Banking.

Below
Sleep Spaces
A personal project inspired by dreaming, surrealism, and the poetry of Robert Desnos. Photography by Catherine Losing.

Below Right
Owen in his studio.

Owen Gildersleeve is a designer, papercraft illustrator and set maker. His illustrations often play with light and shadow, frequently combining multiple-layered paper-cuts with graphical forms and hand-rendered typography. He also enjoys collaborating with photographers, animators, and stylists to help bring his ideas to life. Owen's playful, handcrafted creations won him a prestigious ADC Young Guns 9 award in 2011, and have seen him produce illustrations and designs for an array of international clients. His work has been exhibited in London, New York, and Tokyo. A University of Brighton graduate, he is now based in London where he works from a shared studio.

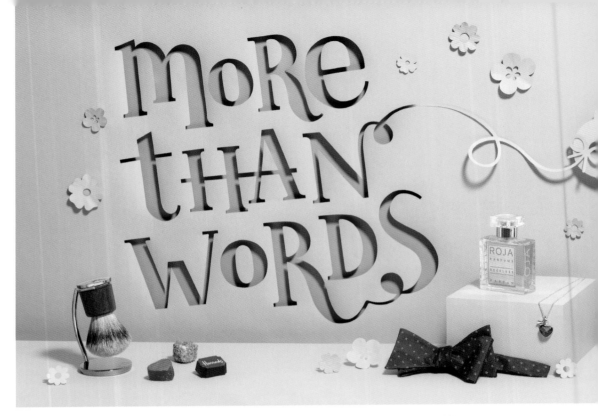

Right
More than Words
Set design for Harrods' Valentine's Day online boutique. Photography by Sam Hofman.

Left
Wallpaper* Portraits
A set of contributor portraits for the 2013 edition of *Wallpaper* Handmade*.

Right
Green Giants?
An illustration for *Bloomberg BusinessWeek* accompanying an article about Big Oil's push towards renewable energy.

Left
Wifi Pixels
A poster campaign for
TFL advertising Wifi
on the Underground.
Photography by
Emma Job.

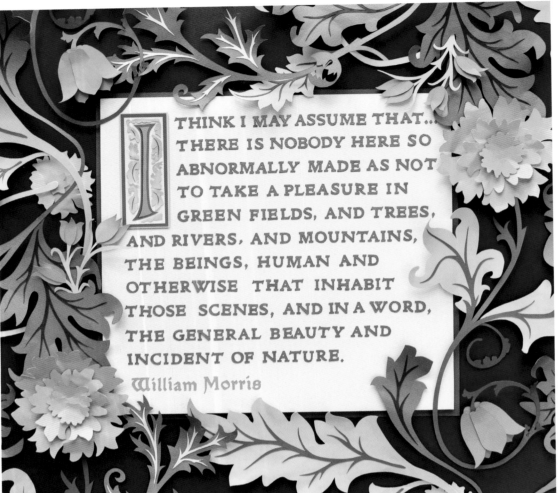

I THINK I MAY ASSUME THAT... THERE IS NOBODY HERE SO ABNORMALLY MADE AS NOT TO TAKE A PLEASURE IN GREEN FIELDS, AND TREES, AND RIVERS, AND MOUNTAINS, THE BEINGS, HUMAN AND OTHERWISE THAT INHABIT THOSE SCENES, AND IN A WORD, THE GENERAL BEAUTY AND INCIDENT OF NATURE.

William Morris

Right
The iPad Explosion
An illustration for the cover of *Computer Arts'* iPad Design Guide, featuring a handmade paper iPad bursting with creativity. Photography by Sam Hofman.

Incident of Nature
An illustration for the Royal Mail's Year Book, to introduce a chapter on the William Morris stamp collection.

Contributors

Acknowledgments

I'd like to say a huge thank you to everyone who helped make this project happen. Firstly, thanks to all the artists involved in this book. I really appreciate your patience in dealing with my constant questions and requests. I'd also like to thank Chris Clarke for helping design the book and for pushing me not to cut corners, Nick Redgrove for his copywriting and proofreading expertise, Evan Gildersleeve and Willis Redgrove for their assistance in collating the work, Uncle John for his guidance and Mum, Dad, and Ciara for their love and support. Finally, I'd like to thank everyone at Rockport Publishers, especially Emily Potts, Heather Godin, John Gettings, and Cora Hawks, for helping me put this book together and for trusting me with this project. You're the best!

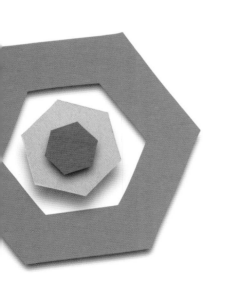

Owen Gildersleeve
London, UK
owengildersleeve.com

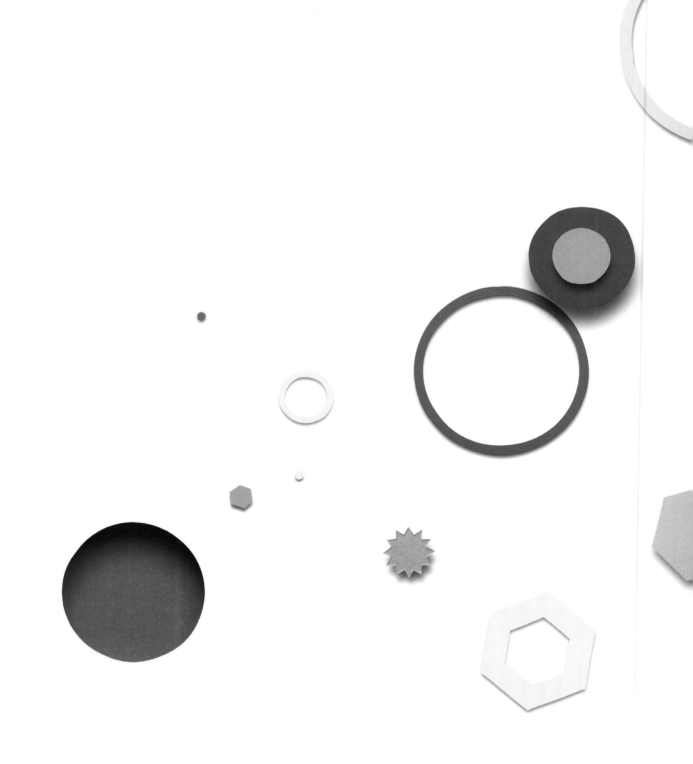